Twayne's United States Authors Series

Sylvia E. Bowman, *Editor*

INDIANA UNIVERSITY

Caroline Gordon

Caroline Gordon

By W. J. STUCKEY
Purdue University

 200

Twayne Publishers, Inc. :: New York

For Elizabeth, Sarah, and John

Preface

Caroline Gordon states in her instructive book *How to Read a Novel*:

The reader who wants to read understandingly—whether he is reading *War and Peace* or the admirable detective stories of Raymond Chandler—must perform an act of self-abasement. He must lay aside his own opinions for the time being, and ask himself not why Mr. Chandler or Count Tolstoi didn't write the kind of book he would like to see them write, but what kind of book they have actually written. That is, he must try to understand what the fiction writer has accomplished before he allows himself to express an opinion on how—or why—he went about accomplishing it.

This advice is excellent for the critic, as well as for the general reader; and I have tried to follow it. It may be that I have not been as objective as I have wished or that blind spots have kept me from seeing my way clearly, but I have attempted to lay aside opinions long enough to discover what the novels and stories of Caroline Gordon are saying. I have also tried to avoid that most alluring of all critical sins: the desire to display my own sensibility at the expense of my subject. It will be for the reader to judge, of course, how well I have succeeded.

My approach in this study has been primarily explicative, a method that is in keeping with the spirit of Miss Gordon's critical approach to fiction in general, with the nature of her own fiction, and also with my own predispositions. For each of the novels and the major short stories I summarize the action and attempt to give some sense of their literal reality; but, in the main, I focus on how the book or short story in question "works", what the major issues are; and, finally, how it relates to other of Miss Gordon's fictions.

As for the arrangement of this book, I give essential biographical facts, summarize my author's comments on fiction, and then discuss her novels in the order of publication. I reserve discussion of the short stories for the latter part of the book, and ignore chronology in order to consider them in the way that seems most pertinent, according to subject or by theme. In the final chapter, I attempt

Preface

to place Caroline Gordon's fiction in some kind of critical perspective—to her times and to the prevailing literary situation. My judgments, it should be said, are not meant to be definitive or final.

It is a pleasure to acknowledge publicly the assistance of those who have helped me in the writing of this book. First of all, I wish to thank Caroline Gordon for invaluable assistance, both direct and indirect, particularly during the year she was visiting writer-in-residence at Purdue University (1963–64). I must make it clear, however, that, though I have benefited from conversation with Miss Gordon, we rarely spoke of her fiction, which she rightly held to be its own best expositor. As the reader will see, I have acknowledged specific indebtedness to her in footnotes. I wish also to thank friends and colleagues of the Purdue University English Department who have taken time from busy schedules to read parts of my manuscript. Michael Yetman proofread several chapters and offered a number of useful suggestions for changes. Robert L. Lowe gave valuable advice for stylistic revision of the early chapters and also helped track down some elusive information. To Harold Watts I owe a special thanks, not only for the interest that he has taken in this study but for the care with which he read several chapters and for his helpful and incisive comments. To A. A. DeVitis for help in reading proof. And to Sylvia Bowman, General Editor of this series, for her efficient and thorough editing.

I also thank Charles Scribner's Sons and Harcourt, Brace Jovanovich for permission to quote from Caroline Gordon's novels and short story collections and Viking Press for permission to quote from *How to Read a Novel*. To Purdue Research Foundation I am grateful for a summer grant that enabled me to begin work on this study. Finally, I wish to thank my wife, June, who helped so much, particularly during the later stages of the writing.

W. J. STUCKEY

Purdue University

Contents

Chronology

1895   Caroline Gordon born October 6, 1895, on Merry Mount Farm, Todd County, Kentucky, daughter of James Morris and Nancy Meriwether Gordon.

1916   Bachelor of Arts degree Bethany College, Bethany, West Virginia.

1920–   Reporter for the *Chattanooga News*.
1924

1924   In New York. Writes for a newspaper syndicate; serves as secretary to Ford Madox Ford; marries Allen Tate, November 2; divorced 1959.

1928   Goes abroad on Allen Tate's Guggenheim fellowship; in England and France.

1929   Awarded a Guggenheim Fellowship in creative writing; in England and France. Serves as Ford Madox Ford's secretary in Paris.

1931   *Penhally*.

1934   "Old Red" wins an O. Henry short story award. *Aleck Maury, Sportsman*.

1935   Publishes *Aleck Maury* in London as *Pastimes of Aleck Maury, The Life of a True Sportsman* (the title she preferred).

1937   *None Shall Look Back*, February; *The Garden of Adonis*, October.

1938   *None Shall Look Back* (a story of the American Civil War) in London. Serves as the first writer-in-residence at Women's College, University of North Carolina.

1941   *Green Centuries*.

1944   *The Women on the Porch*.

1945   *The Forest of the South*.

1946   Doctor of Letters degree, Bethany College, Bethany, West Virginia.

1947   Received into the Catholic Church.

1950   *The House of Fiction*, edited with Allen Tate.

1951   *The Strange Children*.

1952   *The Strange Children* in London. Lectures at the University of Kansas.

1954   Walker Ames Lecturer, University of Washington, Seattle.

1956   *The Malefactors.*

1957   *How to Read a Novel.*

1960   Second edition of *The House of Fiction,* edited with Allen Tate.

1962–   Writer-in-residence, University of California, Davis. *Old*
1963   *Red and Other Stories*

1963–   Writer-in-residence, Purdue University. Doctor of Letters,
1964   St. Mary's College, South Bend, Indiana.

1965   "Cock Crow," a section of *A Narrow Heart: The Portrait of a Woman,* a novel in progress, was published in the summer issue of the *Southern Review.*

1966   Doctor of Letters, Purdue University. Receives $10,000 grant from the National Council of Arts.

1968–   "A Walk with the Accuser (Who is the God of this World)"
1969   in the winter *Transatlantic Review* and "Cloud Nine" in the October–December *Sewanee Review,* sections of a novel in progress.

CHAPTER 1

A Portrait of the Artist

SINCE Ford Madox Ford's enthusiastic praise of *Penhally* in 1931, Caroline Gordon has been a name high on the list of important American writers. Although Ford's high opinion of Miss Gordon's first novel helped bring her to the notice of serious readers, her fiction itself has made secure her reputation as a writer of indisputable merit. Novels such as *Aleck Maury, Sportsman, The Women on the Porch,* and *The Strange Children* were well received in journals and periodicals; and the reputation of these books—all now out of print and generally unavailable—has lingered on. Also, her short stories such as "Old Red," "The Captive," and "Her Quaint Honor," which originally appeared in small-circulation magazines, have been reprinted in widely circulated anthologies; their inclusion has helped establish Caroline Gordon's reputation in schools and colleges as an important short-story writer. In recent years, we also find Miss Gordon's name appearing in literary histories as a writer significantly involved in the Southern literary renaissance.

Despite the praise, the reputation, and the acknowledged importance of Miss Gordon's work, her fiction has not received the kind of critical attention one might have expected it to attract, particularly in an age so productive of literary criticism. To date, there has been only one thin pamphlet and a half-dozen or so articles about Caroline Gordon's eight novels and her two collections of short stories. One reason Miss Gordon's fiction has not attracted much critical attention is that her novels have never been popular; for, though we may prefer to think there is no significant connection between book sales and critical acclaim, popular "serious" writers like John Steinbeck and Ernest Hemingway have received more critical attention than their books require. But among other reasons that Caroline Gordon has been ignored is the fact that she is a demanding writer. Most of her novels are difficult to read, not because they are all stylistically or intellectually complex, but because they demand moral and esthetic responses that many readers are unable to make. They are vigorously "dramatic" books that require of readers almost as much talent in the art of reading as their author has lavished on the art of their writing. Furthermore, as we shall see, Miss Gordon's fiction, though rigorously modern in technique is rigorously antimodern in attitude.

I   Origins and Formal Education

Caroline Gordon was born on Merry Mount Farm in Todd County, Kentucky, on October 6, 1895. Her mother, Nancy Meriwether, was a Kentuckian; her father, James Morris Gordon, was born in Louisa County, Virginia. In the 1880's, Gordon had come to Kentucky as a tutor in the Meriwether family. Later, he conducted a classical school for boys in Clarksville, Tennessee, a town close to the farm where his daughter Caroline was born. Merry Mount Farm and Clarksville (which often becomes Gloversville in Caroline Gordon's fiction) and the surrounding country are the scene of the first four of Miss Gordon's novels and also of a number of her short stories.[1]

Caroline Gordon's formal schooling began under unusual circumstances. For a time she was educated at home, but when she was ten years old she was sent to her father's classical school in Clarksville, where she was the only girl pupil. It was not until she reached high-school age that she officially attended school, in Wilmington, Ohio. Miss Gordon has said: "I remember the first time I was called on to translate a passage in Caesar's *Gallic Wars*. I read it easily, of course, having been put at my Latin at the age of ten, as I recall. The fact that I translated the passage as if it presented no difficulties coupled with my Southern accent set the class into an uproar. Even the teacher laughed until tears came into her eyes. I was never able to translate a passage smoothly after that. I watched the others and went at it the same way they did." [5]

After high school, Miss Gordon attended Bethany College in West Virginia and received the bachelor of arts degree in 1916; and she has received honorary degrees from Bethany (1946), Saint Mary's College (1965), and Purdue University (1966). Among the memories Miss Gordon brought away from her undergraduate days was the intensive reading she was obliged to give the Greek classics. "It is my firm conviction," she has said, "that I learned how to write fiction at Bethany College in 'third-year'

Greek, when Professor Frank Roy Gay (later fired for 'having his head in the clouds') was going on and on, interminably, it seemed to me about that carpet or tapestry upon which Agamemnon walked to his death. For me it was 'the figure in the carpet'— although I didn't remember his interpretation of that scene until many years afterwards." [6]

II *Learning the Art of Fiction*

Caroline Gordon's career as a writer began in journalism, as have the careers of many other American novelists. From 1920 to 1924, she was a reporter for the *Chattanooga News;* and, though the kind of writing she did for this newspaper was of little value to her as a fiction writer, the association was responsible for a significant change that both her personal and professional life were to take. In the *Chattanooga News,* February 10, 1923, she commented on the work of the Fugitives in Nashville, who were just beginning to attract critical attention.[2] What influence the writings of the Fugitives had on Miss Gordon's own work is not yet clear, but certainly some of her views, particularly on agrarianism, are similar to those expressed in that famous collection of essays *I'll Take My Stand* (1930).[3] Miss Gordon's comments on the Fugitives brought her to the attention of members of that group, among them Allen Tate, whom she met and later married. Miss Gordon's marriage to Tate, the poet and literary critic, was to be of great importance in her development as a fiction writer.[4]

Caroline Gordon's more conscious education in the writing of fiction began when she first met Allen Tate. Tate was one of her first teachers, and there is no doubt that his taste and insights— particularly those regarding the artistic effectiveness of dramatizing emotion—helped shape Miss Gordon's development as a writer. Another of her early teachers was Ford Madox Ford, whom the Tates met in New York and for whom Miss Gordon served briefly as a secretary in 1924, shortly before the Tates went abroad. During this time Miss Gordon wrote a story which she showed to Ford; when he read it, she reports, he said merely, " 'Humph, that's ver' nice.' "I realized later," she says, "what was the matter with it. It was not a story. Nothing happened. Like many first efforts it was simply *about* a character."[7]

Later, in the winter of 1924–25, the Tates met Ford again in Paris; and, after their friendship had been re-established, he asked Miss Gordon to help him with his typing. One day, when she appeared as usual and took her place before the typewriter, he asked whether she was doing any writing herself. Miss Gordon said, "I told him I had a novel about a third written but saw that I would have to throw it away. Whereupon he made me vacate the desk and sat him down and took my dictation. That is, he asked, 'What were you going to say next?' and when I told him he would say, 'That is a beautiful sentence. I will take it down.' He took things down for several weeks. By that time I was ready to start back writing my novel. It was really a very generous thing for Ford to have done," Miss Gordon said, "a fine example of the extraordinary generosity he showed young writers if he thought they had the stuff." [8]

In learning to write fiction well and in developing the fine lucid style for which she has been justly praised, Caroline Gordon served a long apprenticeship. It was not until 1929 that she had a story she considered worthy of publication, "Summer Dust," which appeared in *Gyroscope,* a little mineographed magazine edited by Yvor Winters.[9] Though the story was not as tightly constructed as some of her later stories were to be, it was, nevertheless, a beautifully finished piece of writing. A second story appeared in 1930; and in 1931 her first novel, *Penhally,* was published. During the next forty years Miss Gordon published seven more novels and two collections of short stories. She has been at work on her ninth novel, *A Narrow Heart: The Portrait of a Woman,* unpublished as of this writing.

III   *Criticism and Teaching*

In addition to her fiction, Miss Gordon has also published a book of criticism, *How to Read a Novel,* and with Allen Tate she has edited a collection of short stories to illustrate a method of reading fiction, *The House of Fiction.* Miss Gordon, who has also taught in a number of colleges and universities in various parts of the United States, has established a reputation as a distinguished teacher. For years she conducted courses in the novel and the short story at Columbia University, and she has served as a writer-in-residence at several American universities, including the University of California at Davis and Purdue University.

Despite her long experience in teaching courses in creative writing—or perhaps because of it—Miss Gordon has come to feel that the emphasis in such courses is usually misplaced. She believes that students are often encouraged to write before they have a clear notion of what a short story or a novel is. As a consequence, much of her instruction has been devoted, in reality, to teaching the reading of fiction to those who hope someday to be able to write fiction well.

IV *Tradition and the Individual Talent*

However, Caroline Gordon is not primarily a teacher or a literary critic. She is a writer of fiction who has incidentally taught classes in creative writing and who has occasionally turned her hand to criticism. Her interest in criticism is very closely related to her lifelong study of the craft of fiction. To write fiction well, she believes, one must obviously have talent and something to say; but one must also learn how to turn that material into effective stories. To do that, one must study the techniques of fiction as these are revealed to the practiced eye in the works of the masters. The soundness of Miss Gordon's views are obvious to anyone who has seriously attempted to write, for fiction has its craft as well as its mysteries.

However, Miss Gordon's concern with the art of writing fiction has been more than unusual: it has over the years taken on the aspect of something approaching religious devotion. Her aim, to state it very simply, has been to efface herself as a person as completely as she can, to get herself out of her writing, and to allow her story to tell itself. This aim has engaged her in the constant study of how to make her fictions say what she wishes to say without making their author visible to the reader. Such devotion, of course, exacts its toll. A writer who strives not only for excellence but also for impersonality necessarily alienates readers who care more for sentiment than for art. Moreover, a writer who does not exploit or embody in his work the popular myths of his age is not likely to attract much notice from reviewers.

Indeed, the whole direction of Caroline Gordon's fiction runs counter to the main drift of contemporary American literature. Her heroes are neither rebels against society nor self-satisfied exploiters of that society. Whatever rebellion there may be in her fiction is against whatever dehumanizes and perverts traditional human relationships. Like her fellow Southerner William Faulkner, Caroline Gordon is a traditionalist in the modern world. If she seems out of touch with what are called "current realities," that is because her window in the house of fiction looks out upon the world from a somewhat remote and more elevated position than do the windows of her contemporaries. Her vantage point includes a wide view of the past as well as of the present; in fact, we might say that, for her, all experience is contemporaneous and that her interest as a writer is in making whatever action she chooses to deal with come alive in a theater of eternity. The social and political issues which preoccupy some writers are, for her, simply part of "the enveloping action" of her story. To regard her as a conservative, then, is merely to tag her work with an irrelevant label; for her, fiction is universal, not temporal; her concern is with human emotions, not political opinions.[11]

If Caroline Gordon stands apart from what appears to be the mainstream of contemporary American fiction, she nevertheless has something in common with the best writers of this age as well as of ages past. Obviously, she has learned a great deal from Gustave Flaubert, Henry James, and James Joyce about the art of fiction; and there are also points of similarity between her work and that of Ernest Hemingway and William Faulkner. The impersonal tone and the objective quality of her early short stories, for example, remind us of Hemingway's early manner; her rural settings and clear dislike of commercial civilization suggest a kinship with Faulkner.[12] Though an awareness of influences and similarities may help place Miss Gordon in a tradition, it does little to illuminate her work; for those influences have been fully absorbed. What she learned from other writers was chiefly a method of writing, a way of creating an illusion of reality, of constructing scenes, of putting sentences together. Similarities between the world of her fiction and that of Faulkner's and other Southern writers are inevitable since all are writing about the same general region; but the South that Caroline Gordon writes about is as much the creation of her unique imagination as an actual physical place.

In short, it may be said that, though Caroline Gordon can be related to other writers, to movements, to ideologies, and to geographical regions, her fiction almost defies categorizing. She is an artist writing in a tradition large enough and various enough to include Sophocles, Dante, Flaubert, Mark Twain, Chekhov, Henry James, Stephen Crane, and James Joyce. To consider her simply as an illuminator of rural Tennessee and Kentucky is to limit too severely her frame of reference. Her tragedies may be laid in these geographical regions; but, to adapt a phrase from William Faulkner, they also grieve on universal bones.

CHAPTER 2

A Theory of Fiction

CAROLINE Gordon began writing fiction during an era now called by literary historians the "Southern literary renaissance," a period that extends from around 1920 up to the present. The early decade of this "revival" was characterized by a rejection of the old sentimental and romantic attitudes toward the Southern past, an attraction to the formalist movement in poetry begun by T. E. Hulme and the Imagists, a rejection of the idea of progress and industrialism as an answer to Southern problems, and a defense of agrarianism as the only meaningful way of life, not just for the South but also for the North.[1] In poetry, the chief influence was T. S. Eliot; in fiction, the important figures were Gustave Flaubert, Henry James, and James Joyce. The influence of these writers was, of course, not confined to Southern novelists, for Ernest Hemingway and F. Scott Fitzgerald, to mention two important midwesterners, were also deeply influenced by theories like Eliot's "objective correlative" and by the movement toward a tightly controlled, highly compressed, and impersonal fiction. "Render rather than state," "Find the exact word not an approximate one," "Keep oneself as author outside of one's story or novel," and "Dramatize! Dramatize!," were some of the important ideals of the new fiction; and Caroline Gordon was to some extent influenced by them all.

It was, of course, through the Southern group that Caroline Gordon was first introduced to the modern movement in literature; but other influences made themselves felt as she grew and developed. Some of these were living writers whom Miss Gordon knew personally and from whom she received instruction, but others were authors whom she had read and whose theories and examples she adopted for her own uses and from whom she gradually evolved theories about how fiction ought to be written. It is important to emphasize that Caroline Gordon has never tried to be an academic critic. Her interest in criticism is entirely practical, and her critical writings are explications of a method of writing fiction rather than an attempt to understand writers from the standpoint of intellectual history.

As a literary critic, Miss Gordon is not consciously philosophical. There are, of course, philosophical implications underlying her theories of fiction, but they do not concern her. She is aware that she has been influenced by her times, but she accepts that as a necessary limitation. Subsequent ages may view these matters differently, but for her what we believe about fiction is true as far as we are able to see it. Miss Gordon has also remarked that there is little that is original in her critical theories. "What I have learned about the writing of fiction I have gotten from someone else," she has said.[2] And in her view that is as it should be. Really new discoveries in the art of fiction are rare in any age, and only the giants have made them. All that a lesser writer can do is to follow in the footsteps of the masters. And yet, if Miss Gordon has not produced any new theories of fiction, she has nevertheless managed to synthesize a number of diverse and, in some ways, seemingly divergent ideas about writing.

Caroline Gordon's theories about the writing of fiction are chiefly contained in the appendix of the short-story anthology that she published in collaboration with Allen Tate, *The House of Fiction*, and in a collection of essays delivered at the University of Kansas in 1952 and later published as *How to Read a Novel.* These two works, as we shall see, propound certain ideas about fiction that can be illustrated by Miss Gordon's own fiction. These ideas do not, however, tell us everything there is to know about her fictional world; indeed, there is a great deal they do not tell us, for her chief critical concern is not with *what* fiction ought to say about human experience but with *how* it should be said. To be sure, the kind of fiction Miss Gordon prefers would exclude the possibility of doing things that some other writers have attempted to do; but, in her view, those things ought not to have been attempted at all.

I   *What Fiction Is and Is Not*

Caroline Gordon contends that novels and short stories are not slices of life, extensions of an author's personality, or mirror images of reality. They are contrivances of an illusion—or, as Henry James said of the novel, they are "direct personal impression[s] of life." [3] A work of fiction may have its origins in a writer's personal experience, but a successful novel is shaped consciously or unconsciously according to some principle of composition: certain details and incidents are selected; others are rejected in accordance with that principle. Some novels, like those of Charles Dickens, achieve enormous popularity in their own day because they appear to mirror the realities of their time; but the mark of great fictions, whether they achieve popularity in their own epoch or not, lies in the quality of their art. In all good fiction, "from Sophocles and Aeschylus down to a well-contructed nursery tale," there are certain artistic "constants." [4]

Miss Gordon's principal source for those "constants" is Aristotle's *Poetics*, which she says is as valuable to the reader of fiction as it is to the playwright, for "what he says about the play as an art form is equally true of the novel." [5] Aristotle's definition of a play as "the imitation of an action of a certain magnitude might be used to define the novel as an art form." [6] The action in all great fictions conforms to the same pattern Aristotle found in the plays of Sophocles: there are two main divisions of the action, the complication and the resolution; and, though the dividing line between these parts in any complex work is never absolutely distinct, the discerning critic is able to see that the complication is everything from the beginning of the action up to the point just before there is a change in the fortunes of the hero and that the resolution is everything from the beginning of the change to the end of the action. "In a well constructed work of fiction, Complication and Resolution interlock so closely that the casual reader is not conscious of them separately, but in a true masterpiece more than that is accomplished. The Resolution is foreshadowed in the Complication." [7] In some novels and short stories, as in some Greek tragedies, there will also be a peripety: "the change from one state of things in the play to its opposite of the kind described." "We sometimes use the word 'inevitable' in describing such a Peripety. When we do that we pay an author one of the highest compliments. We mean that he has contrived such a completely lifelike illusion that for the moment we are deceived into taking it for life itself." [8]

The resolution of a novel must be foreshadowed in the complication and be as close to the beginning as possible; and, of course, the complication of an action must be resolved in the novel. If it is not, no matter how well written or what good technical effects there are, the work will fail as a novel. Miss Gordon's insistence that the novel is an imitation of an *action* prompts her to exclude from the category "novel" the so-called novel of ideas and to label as failures modern works of fiction in which the hero thinks but does not act. Her insistence on the Aristotelian structure of complication-resolution results in her conclusion that Albert Camus' novel *The Fall (La Chute)* is ultimately a failure "because though in this story the complication of the action progresses beautifully and with seeming inevitability toward its resolution—the action is never resolved." [9]

Another master whose literary insights Miss Gordon incorporates into her theory of fiction is Dante. Adopting the "four-fold method" by which the various symbols in a literary work fuse to convey the author's meaning, as Dante explains them in his *Convito*, Miss Gordon maintains that every good fictional work must have at least two distinct levels of meaning: a *literal* and an *allegorical* (sometimes imprecisely called "the symbolical level"); and in any masterpiece (even of realism) the action will operate on a third level as well, the *Moral*.[10] By literal level is meant not a plausible everyday reality (such as William Dean Howells seems to have meant in his well-known but vague definition of Realism), but rather specific concrete action in a self-contained, fully created world. Thus a story like Franz Kafka's "Hunter Graccus" ("Jaeger Graccus") and a fairy tale like Hans Christian Andersen's "The Snow Queen" are, fictionally speaking, neither fantasies nor allegories; rather, they are stories with a literal level of action that points toward an allegorical and moral level as well.[11]

II *Fiction and Morality*

Unlike other forms of discourse such as poetry, the novel by its nature deals with the conduct of life.[12] This being true, the successful novelist cannot avoid dealing with human relationships. A successful novel, moreover, presents an illusion of life that is consistent with traditional moral behavior; and by *traditional* is meant the tradition of the Western world. Certain acts, such as murder and incest, have always been regarded as immoral in Western societies. The writer who presents them either as moral or as morally neutral courts disaster in his fiction. If he tries to avoid human relationships or if he perverts them, as André Gide does, he succeeds only in writing badly flawed fiction. Even as talented a writer as Guy de Maupassant produced superficial stories because he was blind to the "moral nature of man." [13]

III *The Dramatic Aspect of Fiction*

Although Miss Gordon goes back to Aristotle and Dante for

some of her most important fictional "constants," she also draws heavily on a more recent writer and "scholar of the novel," Henry James; for, while there has been no significant change in the structure and the symbolic method of fictional art since the Middle Ages, there has been technical progress made in the development of the short story and the novel. Samuel Richardson, who "is generally thought of as the father of the English novel," not only "achieves [in *Clarissa*] the immediacy which is the goal of every serious novelist, but, like all the great innovators, paves the way for the triumphs of writers who came after him." In *Clarissa*, Richardson lays the groundwork for the triumphs of Henry James and the 'stream of consciousness' which stood James Joyce in such good stead in *Ulysses*." [14]

The achieving of immediacy is closely bound up with the whole problem of authority or center of vision; and Richardson, though he struggled with this problem in *Clarissa*, only partially solved it. It remained for Gustave Flaubert, writing in the middle of the nineteenth century, to grapple with this problem and to "solve it in a way which had not been used before." [15] Flaubert did so by "evolving a viewpoint" which Miss Gordon calls "the effaced narrator," a device that enabled him to maintain "with an almost incredible agility, the vantage point that is best suited to the moment he is rendering." [16] By means of this device, he could stand far enough away from his heroine to view her with detachment; or he could stand so close at Emma's elbow that, when she looks into a mirror, he could report not only what she sees but things that she herself could never observe.

Gustave Flaubert also made another important technical discovery which, in the view of Allen Tate, established him as the founder of the modern novel: the discovery and perfection of what Mr. Tate and Miss Gordon have called "symbolic naturalism." [17] By *naturalism* is not meant philosophical Naturalism, of course, or even simple Realism, but the use of objects from the natural world to dramatize emotional states. In scenes such as the famous one in which Emma receives a letter of dismissal from her lover Rudolph and carries it up to the attic, Flaubert does not *tell* us how Emma feels when she reads her lover's letter; he renders her anguish by showing us her reactions to the heat of the attic, and to the sight of the weathercocks on the neighboring houses to the very cobblestones of the village square, which, as she looks down at them, seem to be rising up to meet her. . . ." [18] Flaubert did not invent this device for achieving immediacy, Miss

Gordon remarks, but he was "the first to use it consistently for a conscious purpose, and by so doing he has put all novelists who came after him in his debt." [19]

It was Henry James, the great American writer of the late nineteenth and early twentieth centuries, who fully solved the whole vexing problem of achieving dramatic immediacy while at the same time maintaining the flexibility characteristic of the omniscient point of view. He did this by evolving what Percy Lubbock calls "the viewpoint of the central intelligence," [20] a device that enabled him to achieve the immediacy of the first-person point of view without having to surrender to the limitations of that point of view. It also enabled him and the writers who followed after him to write fiction that was almost entirely *dramatic*—fiction in which almost nothing had to be told or explained by the author.

Miss Gordon does not condemn or dismiss fiction that is not entirely dramatic, but she does admire tremendously the novels and stories in which the dramatic effect is fully achieved; and she regards the history of modern fiction as a gradual movement away from the expository method of telling a story to the dramatic rendering we find in James Joyce's masterpiece, "The Dead." For her, the best fiction is that which, while falling almost unnoticed into the traditional form of complication and resolution, also gives the impression that it is not a story that is being told but a drama being "acted out as if on a stage"—or, more accurately perhaps, being unfolded the way life itself is revealed to us.[21] Characters in such fiction, she writes, "not only reveal themselves to us by what they themselves say and do but are further revealed by being shown to us through the eyes of their families, their friends, their enemies, and their acquaintances." [22]

IV *The Proper Hero of Fiction*

In *The House of Fiction,* Miss Gordon pretty much confines herself to statements about techniques of writing fiction; in *How to Read a Novel,* she ventures however, onto more controversial ground and specifies the kind of men who can and can not be the heroes of novels, the kinds of subjects that are suitable for fiction and those that are not. About the proper hero of fiction she argues that, since a novel is an imitation of an action and since characters can only be revealed by what they do, the hero must necessarily be a man who acts. And, traditionally, he is a man who "has certain characteristics and is faced always with the same task: the overcoming of evil that good may flourish." [23]

To Miss Gordon, Mathieu Delarue of Jean Paul Sartre's *Age of Reason* is not a suitable hero because he is incapable of acting and, also, because he is concerned about no one but himself. A character like Delarue, whose "aim is expression, without need of either conscience or motive, is not a real hero and therefore not a fit subject for artistic creation." In her lecture, Miss Gordon contrasts Sartre's Delarue to Fielding's Tom Jones who is a suitable hero because, for all of his faults and all of his own misfortunes, "he is always ready to drop whatever he is doing to help somebody whose fortunes are lower than his own." [24] The two main characters of Aldous Huxley's *After Many a Summer Dies the Swan* are not suitable heroes because they are too unambitious; they are too much the heroes of "self-expression" whose energies are absorbed in being rather than doing.[25]

V   *The Proper Subject of Fiction*

A dimension found in all great novels, Miss Gordon writes, even those like Stephen Crane's *The Red Badge of Courage* and Herman Melville's *Moby Dick* in which no female character appears, is the romatic relationship between a man and a woman.[26] A novel like André Gide's *Counterfeiters*, which lacks such a relationship, cannot therefore achieve greatness. The subject of romantic love is closely tied to the matter of the proper hero of fiction. The proper hero is, as we have noted, necessarily a man of action who reaches out to a world outside himself—"that world which, from time immemorial has been personified in the feminine consciousness." [27]

Miss Gordon is well aware that there are critics and writers who would disagree with her, but her reading and her own writing of fiction have convinced her that the theories she has expressed are not only right for her but have proved right for generations of other writers and will continue to prove useful for generations to come. Indeed, the theories are not her own but those of the great masters of the past whose practice is both the source and the proof of the theories. As to the soundness and the adequacy of Miss Gordon's fictional theories, that subject need not concern us. The concern of this book is with the fiction itself; to some extent, how it reflects Miss Gordon's theories; but, more important, *how* and *what* it shows us about the mind and imagination of Caroline Gordon.

CHAPTER 3

The Beginning of the Quest

FIRST novels, even those of our best writers, are often crude, imitative works that are of interest only for the light they shed on the writers' later mature fiction. Caroline Gordon's first novel, *Penhally*, sheds a good deal of light on her later and more difficult fiction; but it is also a successful and well-written novel. There are none of the usual first novel faults: patches of bad writing, careless shifts in tone, or obvious manipulation for meaning's sake; for *Penhally* is a solidly built, fully realized novel. The opening paragraph, for example, is finely turned, lucid prose; and it also sets exactly the mood of the novel and states poetically the course the main action is to take: "The shadows that laced the gravelled walk shifted and broke and flowed away beneath his boot soles like water. He plunged through them as a horse plunges through a shallow stream. Passing the big sugar tree he tapped it smartly with his cane. It must be rotten at the heart by this time, though it did not sound hollow." [1]

To many readers in 1931, *Penhally* might have seemed, however, merely another family-chronicle novel of the type made popular by the fiction of John Galsworthy; and, to some extent, *Penhally* does fit that pattern. It depicts the decline of the Llewellyns, a once energetic and prosperous Tennessee family; and it demonstrates how each generation, though retaining some of the old qualities, becomes less prosperous and less able to change with the changing times. The resemblance to the standard chronicle formula, however, is superficial. Indeed, though *Penhally* can hardly be called a "debunking" novel, it implicitly disputes the major assumptions about history and morality upon which the most popular family-chronicle novels are based. The ordinary family-chronicle novel aims to show the inevitability of change and the necessity for keeping up with the times, but *Penhally* shows that the decline of the Llewellyn's fortunes, though inevitable, is also tragic.[2]

I   *Decline of the Llewellyns*

Part I of *Penhally* begins in 1826 and focuses on a quarrel between Nicholas Llewellyn and his younger brother Ralph. Nicholas
is the son of the Llewellyn who left Virginia, went west in the
latter part of the eighteenth century, and bought the large tract
of land on which the house "Penhally" was built. Since Nicholas
is the eldest son, born and bred in Virginia under the old laws
of primogeniture and entail, he maintains that the "Penhally"
lands have, in effect, been left entirely to him. His brother, Ralph,
who has grown up in Tennessee where these laws have never
obtained, insists that the land should be divided between them.
Nicholas is hot-headed and irascible; and, when Ralph has the
temerity to suggest that the land be divided, Nicholas flies into
a rage and orders Ralph to take his plate, his furniture, and his
servants and leave "Penhally." Ralph leaves; and, except for two
brief confrontations with Nicholas over settling the estate, the
two brothers do not meet face-to-face for almost forty years. Nicholas resolutely refuses to discuss the division of the property with
intermediaries. Ralph busies himself with his own affairs, mainly
the raising of blooded horses on land that he has bought across
the road from "Penhally."

Since Nicholas never marries and, consequently, has no direct
heirs, he wills the land to the son of a third brother who had gone
farther west to Arkansas, a nephew named John Llewellyn who
has all of the best Llewellyn qualities. Part II of the novel deals
with John Llewellyn's tenure as head of the Llewellyn clan and,
to some extent, with his adventures during the Civil War. When
John's son Frank dies at the age of twenty-eight years, the property
is then settled on Frank's eldest son, Nicholas Llewelleyn. With
the passing of the estate to young Nicholas, the history of "Penhally" is brought up to the 1900's.

Part III deals with the most recent history of the family. Frank's
eldest son, Nicholas, who inherits "Penhally," does not like to farm.
Since he is a businessman, he turns the running of the farm over
to his younger brother, Chance, who loves the land more than
anything else in the world. Through a combination of circumstances, including economic conditions unfavorable to farming,
Chance is unable to make money from "Penhally." When a rich
Yankee woman offers Nicholas a large sum of money for the land,
he sells it. Chance and his mother move into an apartment in town.
"Penhally" is remodeled into a hunt club for rich strangers, and

the fertile land that once grew prime tobacco is now planted thick with turf. Chance wants nothing more to do with "Penhally"; but, when he is urged by his fiancée to attend the opening-night celebration of the new hunt club, he goes. But, before leaving home, he slips a pistol into the pocket of his evening jacket. At the club that night, when he is taunted by his brother Nicholas, Chance shoots his brother to death.

It would be a mistake to overemphasize the historical implications of *Penhally* and to attempt to read it as an account of how the modern South came into being. But, in order to understand the meaning of Chance Llewellyn's violent action at the end of the novel, we must see what in the past leads to this violence. For one of the intentions of the novel is to trace through the history of this period the causes of the destruction of "Penhally" and the kind of life it exemplifies. Among these causes must be included the discarding of the laws of primogeniture and entail, as well as the Civil War which not only beggared the South but hastened the disintegration of the old land-based human relationships and in time made the South over into an image of the North. These are the main historical causes. A less important one, which is also related to the first main cause, is permitting women to inherit riches without the responsibility that such wealth traditionally carries with it.

Penhally, however, is not primarily an attack on social changes or a lament for an older way of life. Like Sophocles' *Oedipus Rex*, it is a tragedy. The changes in the laws of inheritance, though they took place even before the opening of the novel, are like the breaking of a divinely appointed law; and the consequence is that the land and the men living on it are doomed to live under a curse. The curse has to do with the division of the land, the scattering of the families, and the ultimate perversion of ancient human values. The law cannot be reversed, no expiation can be made, and no cathartic resolution can exist. The heroic individual, who is not himself responsible for the curse, can only hurl himself in senseless fury against his antagonist, who is, ironically, his elder brother.

Penhally is not simply about the defeat of the Old South but about the defeat of a way of life that had the possibility for meaningful and satisfying human relationships. Under the older system, a man did not inherit the land to do with as he pleased; he held it in trust for his family and his descendants. As a consequence of this trust, and always assuming the right kind of character, the inheritor of the land felt a sense of responsibility to those dependent upon him; and, consequently, he expected, sometimes unreasonably, a sense of loyalty from his dependents. The older system however, instead of setting one brother against another, as happens in the modern world, made one brother the head of the family and consigned others to positions of subservience. Naturally, the system did not always seem fair to those excluded from inheriting the land, but it did at least preclude the tragic quarrel that finally ends the Llewellyn dynasty.

In the earlier quarrel between old Nicholas Llewellyn and his brother Ralph, Nicholas never thinks of the land as his own. It is, he thinks, "ours"; and what hurts him is Ralph's unwillingness to share "it all between them" because he must have his own house on his own land. The issue in the quarrel between the two brothers is, simply stated, a quarrel between two different concepts of life; life lived as part of a family relationship in which there are both rights and responsibilities, and life lived as an isolated individual for whom responsibilities exist only to one's self. To be sure, Ralph Llewellyn is more concerned for the welfare of others than is his descendant Nicholas; but Ralph's concern tends to be less personal and more abstract, an attachment to his nation rather than to his clan.

The fate of the two brothers makes clear which is the sounder way of life. Nicholas holds on to his land. Ralph squanders his, indulging his taste for luxury and later, his patriotism by outfitting troops to fight in the war. Frederick P. W. McDowell seems to believe that in this novel the Civil War is shown to be a noble cause.[3] On the contrary, the war is shown to be destructive and divisive, a war launched by landless Southern politicians who had "nothing to lose and everything to win."[4] Ralph's contributions to the Southern cause were generous and high spirited, to be sure; but in the context of his character and in the issues of this novel, they are additional manifestations of his extravagance and lack of responsibility to both his family and his heirs. It is also significant that, in his will, Ralph divides his property between his son and daughter, though there is nothing to divide after his death.

Nicholas Llewellyn, however, not only keeps "Penhally" intact during the war; but, because he converts his currency into gold and buries it in the forest, he also enables his heir, John, to keep the estate going after the war. Such an act in another character and under different circumstances might be reprehensible, but Nicholas Llewellyn's first concern is to save the land that has been put in his trust; and it is his conviction that, if all men had done the same, there would have been no war.[5]

II *The Cause of the Decline*

The tragic end of the Llewellyn line and of "Penhally" is however, not simply the result of historical events. John Llewellyn is wearied by the Civil War in which he fought long and valiantly, and his lassitude seems to him to be reflected in the general weariness and the defeat of the country.[6] The reader sees, however, that, whatever the cause of that weariness, John's personal failures also contribute to the tragedy that overtakes his son and eventually his grandsons. John fails his wife. Exactly how, we are not told; but his wife knows, and he knows; and, as a consequence, he feels guilty. To atone for that guilt, he pays a kind of emotional blackmail by pleasing his wife rather than by acting in his son's best interests: Lucy, John's wife, discovers that their son is in the bedroom of a young female cousin who is visiting them. Lucy's sense of propriety is outraged, and she sends her husband to settle the matter. Instead of handling the situation responsibly, with an eye on the future, he forces his way into the girl's bedroom and precipitates an elopement that begins a marriage that is disastrous for Frank and for "Penhally." The girl, whom John has completely misjudged, is not much better than a prostitute. Frank has to leave home in order to live with her, which cuts him off completely from "Penhally" and eventually leads to his suicide. The marriage also introduces into the Llewellyn strain a fatal corruption.

Modern prejudice to the contrary, *Penhally* shows that what counts in this world is blood, a man's or a woman's breeding. If corruption is admitted into a family, it inevitably appears in succeeding generations. Frank's wife was notoriously promiscuous; and, though the marriage produced one sound son, Chance, the elder son seems to have inherited more of his mother's qualities than his father's. At least, when the real test of his character comes, he is willing to sell out for money. Just as corruption once introduced into a family line crops out, so does fundamental strength of character. Chance inherits his forebears' inbred sense of principle, but he does not inherit the land. And this accident of circumstance, along with the growing corruption of the times, precipitates the tragedy in which the hand of one brother is turned against another.

In popular political discussion, when distinctions are made between liberal and conservative, it is usually said that conservatives are concerned mainly with property rights and liberals with human rights; and the implication is that these are mutually exclusive. Miss Gordon's contention in this novel seems to be that, in the kind of society she is writing about, a concern for land necessarily involves the proprietor (he is not the owner) in a concern for human rights. Men like John and Chance Llewellyn who love the land and have a sense of responsibility to their successors, also have a sense of responsibility to the living. In his will, John provided that "Penhally" was to "offer asylum to infirm and dependent kinsmen and kinswomen. . . ." [7] Also, the family graveyard on "Penhally" land was to be maintained by the heir to the property.

In the modern world, the concept of property ownership is usually bound up with feelings of exclusiveness and personal vanity. Nicholas' wife, a town girl whose father made a fortune in wheat (presumably speculating), cannot stand the thought of her husband's helping Negro servants out of personal difficulties, nor can she abide the thought of relatives burying members of their families in the graveyard her husband maintains at "his" expense. She wants him to circulate a letter telling relatives that they must pay "so much a head" to keep up the graveyard. [8] Chance, of course, immediately feels the rightness of the responsibility to bury the dead and to care for unfortunate kinsmen, even though the land does not belong to him. He also feels the responsibility that his brother owes to a Negro foster brother whose mother had nursed him, Nicholas, when he was a baby and whose own son suffered as a consequence.

The passion for money and selfishness are obviously not modern phenomena, but the passing of the old society based on the land and the rise of the new class have reversed the old values. What used to be considered a serious failing, if not actually a vice, has now become a standard of respectable conduct; and the old concern for the weak and the unfortunate has given way to selfish, monied snobbery. Money—or making money the basis of human relationships—is the sign of modern corruption. This view is shared by other Southern writers, notably William Faulkner; but Miss Gordon's method, like her material, differs from Faulkner's. Whereas Faulkner attempts to overwhelm us with the horrors of Snopesism, Miss Gordon tries to make us see the good qualities of the old order and to feel the tragedy of its destruction.

Indeed, it could be said that the novel is constructed with this end in mind. The first two sections constitute what Miss Gordon calls the complication of the action; the final section, the resolution. The care with which the novel has been constructed can be seen by the way the resolution repeats, in a sense, the old quarrel between Nicholas and Ralph Llewellyn; but the moral position of the two brothers is reversed. It is now the younger brother who loves the land and the older brother who wants to destroy it. In the earlier section, the love of the land preserves it; in the later section, love of the land is not only ineffectual but actually precipitates a murder. This inversion is Miss Gordon's way of dramatizing a moral judgment.

III   The Art of Penhally

The structure, style, selection of incidents, and the tone of *Penhally* are calculated to make us feel the tragedy of the loss of this older way of life. The book is arranged and the action is managed so that the wisdom of the old way is plainly manifest. If old Nicholas Llewellyn had not been reared to believe in the justness of primogeniture and entail and if he had divided the property, the Llewellyn estate would have been squandered in the Civil War. Moreover, if Nicholas Llewellyn in 1930 had not been able to sell the property, "Penhally" would not have been turned into a hunt club, and Nicholas Llewellyn would not have been killed.

The action of the novel, however, does not seem contrived in order to illustrate a thesis. The book convinces in the way that fiction must convince if it is to be successful, by making us believe in the reality of these characters and these events. Miss Gordon's principal technique in the contrivance of this illusion is realistic detail. She makes us see vividly "Penhally," the people, and the life that goes on there. And, if we feel as well as see the reality of the fictional world, that is as much as she asks us to do.

Penhally is an unusually fine first novel. It is somewhat looser and less technically accomplished than Miss Gordon's later fiction, but its freshness still remains undiminished. It is no wonder that, when Ford Madox Ford in 1931 surveyed the promising young American novelists, he should have made *Penhally* a springboard for his discussion.[9] Of course, Caroline Gordon was a protégée of Ford's, but Ford Madox Ford was never prone to give indiscriminate praise. *Penhally* deserved all of the good things that were said about it.

IV *The Hero and the Tradition*

For students of Caroline Gordon's fiction, *Penhally* is especially interesting because it contains themes that appear in later novels. We find in it the tragedy of the Civil War, the destruction of the small farmer, the disintegrative effects of sexual promiscuity—these and other themes that are developed more fully in later fiction are present in *Penhally*. But the most significant thing about the novel is that it marks the beginning of what was to be a lifelong quest in Caroline Gordon's fiction for heroes who would not only embody qualities of courage and bravery but would also display a sense of responsibility for the welfare of other human beings.

Nicholas Llewellyn is the first of such heroes; his nephew John and his great-grandson Chance Llewellyn are paler copies. With the destruction of "Penhally" and the way of life that it represented, the possibility of realizing that kind of heroism was all but finished. From here on Miss Gordon looked in other places for her hero— to the soldier in wartime, to the pioneer on the frontier, to the small farmer fighting the drought, and to the fisherman battling the practical minded, work-obsessed world. Whatever his calling, his time, or his place, Miss Gordon's favorite hero was to be a better-than-average man caught in a situation that brought forth his best qualities. And almost always—and it is this that produces the tragic, the elegiac tone of her fiction—the superior man is destroyed because of his superiority. The cautious or self-seeking man always survives.

In her preoccupation with the tragic hero, Miss Gordon has something in common with other American novelists of her time, but the kinship may have less to do with a common nationality than with a commonly shared culture. For, though Miss Gordon's heroes almost always fit the traditional patterns, as do the protagonists of Hemingway and Faulkner, the nature of her heroes' struggles, their relationship to their societies, and the grounds upon which they are to be pitied are different from those of her countrymen's. In *Penhally*, the career of Chance Llewellyn fits the traditional pattern. He is a better-than-ordinary person who is destroyed by forces that might be said to represent the corrupt values of his society. In this he resembles Frederic Henry of *A Farewell to Arms* and Joe Christmas of *Light in August*. But there is this important difference: Llewellyn is not that popular version of the Romantic hero—the alienated outcast at odds with conventional or respectable society. The conflict is not personal or emotional.

He is not recommended to us because of his capacity to feel more tenderly than those who destroy him. Llewellyn is morally superior because, in the eyes of the author, he represents a superior way of life. His moral value, then, lies more in what he represents than in what he feels as a private person. He is the hero of a culture that has been destroyed, and it is as much the destruction of that culture as the death of the hero that gives the conclusion of *Penhally* its elegiac tone.

CHAPTER 4

The Sportsman as Hero

W HILE critics look for unities and clear-cut lines of development in a writer's work, writers, happily, write what interests them. Caroline Gordon's second novel, *Aleck Maury, Sportsman,* is different both in tone and in method from *Penhally*; and, though it is possible to make significant connections between it and her other novels, it shows a side of her talent and her sensibility not often revealed in her fiction. Aleck Maury, the hero of *Aleck Maury, Sportsman* (1934), more nearly resembles the typical modern hero than any of Miss Gordon's other protagonists. Maury, a rebel of sorts, is a teacher and a husband and father; but his deepest interest is in hunting and fishing. Therefore, much of his life is spent eluding the responsibilities that would keep him from pursuing his pleasure. His greatest triumphs appear to be his successes in escaping from the classroom and from the stratagems of his family, as these attempt to make him spend his hours in ways that he finds uncongenial. Aleck Maury's revolt, however, must be read against the backdrop of *Penhally* and in light of both Maury's character and of the special tone of the novel. Paradoxically, we are not to take his revolt too seriously; but, in another, deeper sense, we are to take it very seriously, indeed.

I *Aleck Maury, Sportsman*

Aleck Maury, Sportsman is a novel in the form of what purports to be a memoir told by the principal character, Alexander Gordon Morris Maury. Maury begins his story with an account of his early life in the Green Springs neighborhood of Louisa County, Virginia, and then shifts to his experiences in Kentucky as a tutor in the Fayerlee family. There Maury marries Molly Fayerlee, the oldest of his pupils, and begins a long and somewhat erratic career as a teacher of the Classics. He teaches first in a private country school; then in a seminary in Gloversville, Tennessee; and then moves on to a small college in Poplar Bluff, Missouri. After his wife's death, Maury retires to a farm in Tennessee and breeds fish. After two years of retirement, he leaves the farm to go to Florida to fish. When the fishing disappoints him, he returns to Tennessee to make his home with his daughter and son-in-law. When Maury quickly discovers that these young people are determined to live in a place that is uncongenial to him, he escapes to a resort, Caney Fork, where life—particularly the fishing—will be much more enjoyable.

On the face of it, *Aleck Maury, Sportsman,* is a loose, episodic book held together by the chronological march of events and by the narrative voice of Aleck Maury as he recalls what are for him significant events from his past. Coon hunts, fox hunts, a trip to the West Coast, and a good many hunting and fishing experiences are recounted with meticulous attention to detail, particularly to the details of fishing. We can see why this book has attracted a special, nonliterary audience of hunters and fishermen; indeed, it would be possible to read it as simply a collection of authentic anecdotes about sport. This episodic quality of the narrative is deceptive, for the events of Maury's life have been carefully arranged to emphasize certain qualities in Maury and to give his story a dramatic structure.

II   *The Structure*

The first-person point of view, as Miss Gordon has asserted, is the most barbarous of all points of view in fiction; for it imposes on the writer the necessity of justifying the narrator's presence in the story while at the same time making him a convincing and reliable authority.[1] Moreover, if the narrator tells a story in which he himself is involved, the question of his authority is always open to question. Many writers, of course, have taken advantage of what might be regarded as the potential for unreliability implicit in the first-person point of view. Miss Gordon herself has exploited this quality in a fine short story, "Her Quaint Honor." [2] But in *Aleck Maury* she has managed to make Maury a reliable narrator and, at the same time, to capitalize on his limitations.

Maury's reliability is established at the beginning of the novel. He has a precise and vivid memory of the important things that have happened to him—that is to say, things concerned with sport. He remembers exactly how a certain gun felt in his hand, how a particular dog behaved, exactly which technique in the art of fishing he learned on a particular stream, and the color and the conditions for fishing certain rivers at certain times of the year. However, Maury fails to remember details about his family; or, if he does remember, he reports them in a half-abstracted, be-mused way. When he describes the stratagems he must employ to allow himself time to hunt or fish, he does so with perfect candor—in the belief that his reader will understand his feeling and his motives exactly. For example, he tells how, when he was teaching school for the Fayerlees, he arranged to hold his classes in the morning so that he could have the afternoons free for fishing.[3] Also, he tells us quite frankly that he left his teaching job at a seminary in Gloversville in order to take one in a college in Poplar Bluff, Missouri, simply to be near the Black River, a stream that he had long wanted to fish.[4]

As a consequence of Maury's candor, of his occasional amuse-ment at himself, his pleasure in outwitting his wife Molly, who is somewhat ambitious for his worldly success, and of his serious and meticulous attention to the minutiae of hunting and fishing lore, there is gradually built up a lightly ironic tone. We see be-yond Maury to the author who is amused and, at the same time, censorious in a mock-serious way. The lightly ironic tone is main-tained throughout almost two thirds of the novel; then, suddenly, the tone becomes somber, even melancholy. Maury's wife dies, and Maury is suddenly forced to confront the most serious crisis of his life. All along, when Molly was alive, he thought of her, half-humorously, as allied with those forces bent on keeping him from his beloved sport. Molly seemed the chief "enemy"—the voice of duty, of reason, and of conscience. With Molly dead, then, libera-tion should follow. Maury should feel himself free at last to live his life as he wishes. But Molly's death has a very different effect: Maury is dejected. Molly's death has brought the hero face to face with the real enemy: fear. When she was alive, Molly had always laughed at Maury's vague, unfounded fears and had called him the biggest coward in the world. At her death, Maury discovers what he has always been afraid of: that his elation, his delight in sport, would go from him.[5]

The novel does not end with this discovery, for *Aleck Maury* is not a tragedy. Maury recovers his delight and is able to escape the oppressive benevolence of his daughter Sally, who shows alarm-ing signs of taking up the battle to subjugate him. The last thirty or so pages of the novel which deal with Maury's recovery are among the most amusing in the book; together, they constitute a sustained comic irony. After Maury is forced to retire from the college at Poplar Bluff, he decides to go somewhere to live out the remainder of his life quietly. For two years he lives on the farm of an old friend in Tennessee and breeds fish in an artificial lake. He becomes a part of the family and is even able to think calmly about his own death—a subject he has never had much relish for. A brief excursion on the Cumberland River, however, brings Maury back to his old love, fishing. He sees Colonel Wyndam, a figure from his young manhood, now ninety years old but still able to climb down to the water every day to fish for channel cat and buffalo.[6]

The encounter with Colonel Wyndam is the turning point of the novel, for it marks the beginning of Maury's recovery. The meeting makes him realize that a man "who had reached the age of ninety has achieved something: he was free from the fear of approaching old age. It was already here. One might return then, in a sense, to the timelessness of childhood. Every day would be a gift from the gods and it would be a man's plain duty to enjoy it."[7] Enjoyment for Aleck Maury, however, is not easily won; for he is a man with high standards. He abandons fish breeding and goes to Florida, where he has been given to understand there is a remarkably fine freshwater lake. The beautiful lake, however— "cypress fringed, clear as air, white sand bottom"—is snarled with eel grass. It is, Maury discovers, an impossible place to fish. This discovery is "one of the bitterest moments of [his] life."[8]

At this moment, disillusioned with Florida and anxious to return to his own part of the country, Maury receives a letter from his daughter Sally. She and her new scholar husband are returning from Europe, and they want him to make his home with them in Tennessee where they will look for a suitable place in the country. Maury joins them in East Tennessee, and the search begins on the Elk River. Maury has in mind the ideal house on the ideal stream—everything conveniently arranged for fishing. But the house Sally and Steve are attracted to, Maury finds unsuitable. To Steve, the house (the Potter house, it is called) is a fine specimen of the "enclosed dog run." To Sally, it has "marvelous" lines and a marvelous mantel. To Maury, it is an old ramshackle affair badly in need of repair on a river that "looks as if it would be muddy for about half of every year."[9] When Maury points this out, the search continues, with Steve driving the car furiously through the mountains and Sally casting long glances back in the direction of the Potter house.

At a filling station in the mountains, when they stop briefly for gas, Maury discovers Caney Fork, a stream in which, a native tells him, "You can ketch most any fish you want." Sally, however, is not impressed with Caney Fork. She is more concerned with the book Steve is writing on Free Trade, and she explains to her father: "You see, Bright and Cobden thought they believed in Freedom and Democracy and all that and they did do a great deal to create anti-slavery sentiment during the Civil War. But Cobden was a very rich textile magnate and his stand against the South was simply a part of the movement of the Capitalist system to crush the power of the source of raw cotton so they could control it." [10]

At this point in her discourse, Maury leans forward and punches Steve in the back. "Stop!" he says. "Stop right here, feller." Steve stops the car, and they all get out in the middle of the new concrete bridge. Maury goes over to the rail and looks down: "The river coming into view between banks covered with cane described a sharp bend, then widened out into a broad still pool. . . . Farther up the water had a perceptible current but here under the bridge it flowed so gently that the eye could hardly detect the movement. And it was of the most lovely pellucid green I have ever looked upon." [11] Steve says, "It's a shame we can't take a couple of days off and fish here." Maury heaves a sigh and says, "No, we'd better be getting on. You can't do any good, fishing, unless your mind's settled." [12]

The search for a house continues until five o'clock that afternoon. Maury, his daughter, and his son-in-law stop for cold drinks at a bus stop restaurant. After they order their second mug of beer, Sally says, "You know, Steve . . . the more I think about that Potter place, the better I like it. I don't believe you'd ever find rooms of such beautiful proportions. And that mantel . . . I don't believe I can live without it." [13] Steve estimates that it would take three months to repair the house so they could move into it. "Three months . . ." Maury says. Sally looks up. "It wouldn't kill you to go without fishing three months," she says. Suddenly Maury hears himself saying, "I'm seventy years old . . . this November I was seventy years old."

But Steve and Sally are too preoccupied with the house to hear him. Sally wonders aloud whether the "portico ought to go back exactly as it was or maybe a little smaller." And Maury sees that he is about to be trapped. It will take all of those months to repair the house so they can live in it. Moreover, it is five hundred feet down to a river that is muddy half of every year. Maury gets up

from the stool and goes outside the restaurant, leaving Sally and
Steve still lost in talk. He sees a bus bearing a sign: Caney Fork.
He pays the driver five dollars to get his suitcases out of Steve's
car and into the bus. "Where you getting off?" the driver asks.
Maury leans back and releases his pent-up breath: "Caney Fork,"
he says.

III   *The Meaning of Sport*

The lightly ironic tone and the comic resolution of the novel
are exactly suited to the story Miss Gordon is telling. They permit
her to do justice to two possible views that may be taken of Aleck
Maury's story and, at the same time, allow her to suggest which
is the right one. The tone and the conclusion acknowledge in a
sense that, from the standpoint of the workaday world, there is
something frivolous and irresponsible about Maury's passion for
sport; but the events of the novel themselves show us that, from
a more elevated point of view, there is something admirable, even
heroic, about Maury. He triumphs over forces that many men
would have succumbed to. He manages to free himself from female
domination and from the work-obsessed world's conception of living.

Aleck Maury's value is not just that he struggles heroically to
live his own life. It is the quality of the life itself that is to be
admired, the life of an educated man who, unlike other members
of his society, has managed to keep alive within him a joyful
response to the natural world. Maury's response to the out-of-doors,
of course, is not a passive romantic exultation in the presence of
majestic nature, nor is there anything transcendental in his love
of field and stream. Though he is occasionally aware of how preoccupied other men are with getting and spending, he is always
surprised by that discovery. Nature is something that he responds
to almost unconsciously. His conscious attention is fixed on the
details of his hunting or fishing; but, in the act of "wetting a line"
or covering a field, he is experiencing the kind of simple pleasure
that, in its literal reality, is unanalyzable joy.

Maury's pleasure in sport unites him with the simpler, more
primitive characters in the book—who are, for the most part, ignorant, uneducated men who share this obsession. Maury, however,
is more than an ordinary fishing enthusiast: he is an artist, not a
romantic artist, to be sure, but the kind of artist Miss Gordon
herself might be expected to admire. He is passionately devoted
to discovering the techniques of fishing and hunting that will make

him a master of these arts. Indeed, for him, the pleasure of a sport comes as much from the mastering as from the exercise of the craft, though ideally the two are joined.

The meaning of *Aleck Maury, Sportsman* goes even deeper. In his passionate response to nature and in his devotion to his craft and to the ritual of fishing, Maury also embodies qualities and attitudes that are traditionally associated with religious devotion. He is a life-long novice, we might say, to the mysteries of nature. Fishing and hunting are his rituals, his means of participating in those mysteries. Though the hunting and fishing are real enough, it is not the fish or the bird that Maury wants. It is the act itself that is valued—the act which, when well performed, combines self-discipline, talent, art, knowledge, and self-abnegation. As a reward for the successful mastery of these, then, comes pleasure as well—not the pleasure of an escape from more important duties into idleness, as the rest of the world imagines—but the kind of pleasure known only to the happy few: the pleasure of performing well an act in which all of the faculties are brought under control and directed toward a higher end.

Andrew Lytle reads *Aleck Maury, Sportsman* largely in regional terms. Lytle suggests that Maury's "dislocation," as he calls it, is caused by the economic and political ruin of the South after the Civil War.[14] Certainly, the Southern background from which Maury has come is important in explaining Maury's origins. The South of pre-"Penhally" days is gone and, along with it, the integrated social order against which Maury might have been measured. Maury, however, lives in the modern world; and it is against it—a money-success-orientated one—that Maury must be seen.

Aleck Maury, then, is not a Southern cultural hero dislocated by the ruin of his native region. He is a man isolated from other men because of an extraordinary responsiveness to the natural pleasures of sport. As Maury observes, most men spend their days at uncongenial occupations and regard life as something to be exchanged for success in business, politics, or intellectual pursuits rather than as something to be enjoyed in its fullest measure. Miss Gordon's book should not be read as a glorification of mere hedonism, nor simply as calling into question the need or value of the serious preoccupations that Aleck Maury rejects. We should read it, in other words, in the same spirit that we read Thoreau's *Walden*: as the picture of one man's life which may in its implications have universal applicability.

Indeed, Aleck Maury is one of a special breed of literary heroes who very early become passionately devoted to a life of sport, a passion—it might be said—that cuts across regional, natural, and racial barriers. Among this small but impressive band, all of whom share to some extent a passion for sport and love of the natural world might be mentioned Isaac Walton of *The Compleat Angler*, William Wordsworth of *The Prelude*, Ivan Turgenev of *The Sportsman's Notebook*, Thoreau of *Walden*, the Mark Twain of *Huckleberry Finn* and of "Old Times on the Mississippi," the solitary fisherman of Yeats' poem, "The Fisherman," and, more recently, Hemingway's Nick Adams of "Big Two-Hearted River."

IV *Aleck Maury's* Uniqueness

Aleck Maury, Sportsman is technically different from the kind of novel Caroline Gordon usually writes; for it is, in the first place, a novel primarily of character. Her heroes do not typically stand apart from the action and live in the reader's memory after the book has been closed. Instead, they sink back into the design of the book and, in retrospect, become part of the dramatic action. We cannot generally recall Miss Gordon's protagonists without at the same time thinking of all the entangling alliances that make them up— the other characters, the houses, the landscapes, even the gestures— and of the important changes that take place between the beginning and the end of the novel. We see them in the flux and flow of time or in the dim web of circumstance; and, for this reason, it is difficult, if not actually impossible, to talk about her protagonists as we can about the characters of William Faulkner.

Aleck Maury, however, has a life and a reality that seems quite independent of either time or circumstance. Indeed, the effectiveness of this novel and the success of Miss Gordon's portrayal of Aleck Maury depend in large part on his ability to thwart both time and circumstance and to remain a free spirit. After putting the book down, we see him still, somewhat bigger than life-sized, loaded down with his rods and fishing gear, and headed for Caney Fork and a life of perpetual sport. It is not surprising that *Aleck Maury, Sportsman* has proved to be Caroline Gordon's most popular novel.

There are doubtless a number of reasons why Caroline Gordon has been so successful in the creation of Aleck Maury. One explanation may be that he is based on her father whom she admired very much and whom she knew in a way she could not know possible prototypes for the male protagonists of her other novels.

Another less obvious but more likely explanation is that there is both more and less of Miss Gordon herself in this novel. Actually, there is little autobiography, much less than in some of her other novels. Sarah and Steven Lewis are, clearly, inspired by Caroline and Allen Tate; but they are oversimplifications and exaggerations of the author and her husband. It is in the creation of Maury that Caroline Gordon has put a great deal of herself. She is not a fisherman nor a hunter, though she has learned a great deal about both; but, like Maury, she is, as we have noted, a disciplined, devoted artist who takes the same delight in perfecting her technique as Maury did his; and her dedication has been just as devout. She writes, ultimately, for the same reason that Maury fished—for the sheer delight of it, not that there isn't also some pain and disappointment. She might have said of Maury, as Flaubert said of his Bovary, "Aleck Maury, *c'est moi.*"

CHAPTER 5

The Soldier as Hero

IN popular American fiction, there appear to be two chief ways of writing about the Civil War. One, the way of the romancer, is to glamorize; the other, the fashion of the "serious" popular novelist is to debunk the romantic myth by showing that the war was brutal and that the motives behind it merely those of economic gain.[1] In *Penhally*, Caroline Gordon dealt with the Civil War only incidentally; but it is significant that her treatment of it differs from both popular traditions. In *Penhally*, the war is not exploited either for swashbuckling excitement or for a journalistic exposé; it is, instead, an historical event that impinges on the lives of her characters.

In her full-length novel about the Civil War, *None Shall Look Back* (1937), Miss Gordon treats the war in somewhat the same way. Her interest is neither in romance nor in debunking; it is in making us see the reality of the war in order to make us believe in and be moved by the tragic outcome of the novel. It is true, as one critic has complained, that Miss Gordon is not concerned in this novel about the injustices of Negro slavery; but then she has never been concerned with problems of injustice in any of her fiction.[2] What concerns her is how a character, black or white, conducts himself in the face of impending disaster.

I *The Use of History*

Caroline Gordon writes about the Southern past because it interests her; provides her with materials; and, more important, it endows her fiction with an authority the present cannot afford: the authority of historical fact. Novels are, in a sense, histories; for, though they are fictions, they convince partly through the reader's willingness to think of them as having happened. A novel set in modern times must somehow come to terms with the widely held myth that life is without meaning and that heroic acts are therefore impossible. Miss Gordon, as we have seen, does not accept this myth; on the contrary, she believes in both the possibility and in the meaning of heroic action. But she is also aware of the difficulties of creating heroes in a world that gives heroism neither credence nor scope. By setting her novels in a time remote from the skeptical present, she can avoid having to confront a view diametrically opposed to her own of the world.

Although Miss Gordon has removed her fictions from the contemporary scene, she does not retire to a never-never land (as the English novelist J. R. R. Tolkien has done) but incorporates into her novels historical events that become part of the enveloping action and historical personages who become paradigms of heroic virtue and help give her fictional heroes plausibility. By creating these historical persons as she would any fictional character, she gains a double authority: that of fictional realism and of historical fact. And heroism, though out of fashion in a post-Freudian world and therefore unconvincing perhaps in a novel about New York, can be convincingly displayed in a novel set in Civil War or Revolutionary times—provided, of course, that the novelist's art works. Miss Gordon's art works very well in her second historical novel, *None Shall Look Back* (1937).

II   *The Characters*

As I have indicated, *None Shall Look Back* takes place during Civil War times, roughly from 1861 through 1865; and the scene is the Kentucky-Tennessee area around Clarksville, Tennessee, where a number of Miss Gordon's novels and stories are set. Some of the action also takes place near Chattanooga; some, in Mississippi and in northern Georgia. Several historical personages appear in the novel, including Robert E. Lee and U. S. Grant; but the most important of these is Nathan Bedford Forrest, the historical paradigm, or "real" hero of the novel. Forrest's military exploits not only give coherence to the chapters dealing with the war, but his character and actions provide much of the novel's meaning.

The first character encountered in *None Shall Look Back* is Fontaine Allard, a gentleman planter whose forebears, we learn, had come to Kentucky from Virginia two generations earlier. Allard, as the novel opens, has just turned sixty-five. He loves his land and thinks of farming as the only respectable way of life. There is also Charlotte Allard, Allard's wife, who manages her household with both competence and relish. There are also their middle-aged daughter Cathy, whose marriage has failed, and their three grandchildren: Jim, who is married to the daughter of a town storekeeper; Ned, who enlists in Forrest's rangers but sits out most of the war in a Northern prisoner-of-war camp; and Lucy Churchill—all of them children of the Allard's daughter Honoria who had died in childbirth.

Among the purely fictional characters, there are also the Rowans, sports-loving cousins of the Allards who live at "Music," a day's ride from "Brackets," where the Fontaine Allards live. There are also the Georgia Allards—Susan Allard and her sons Rives and Miles and her daughter Mitty—who live at "Good Range" in northern Georgia. Susan Allard's husband was killed by a stranger with whom he had generously shared his horse. Susan Allard maintains that her husband had been right to share his horse even though it resulted in his death. Vengeance, she says, belongs to the Lord. Susan Allard gives away her worldly possessions and brings up her children to work hard and to "do good." She believes that manual labor is salutary and makes her sons and foster-sons work half of every day in the fields with the Negroes. As a consequence of the self-sacrificing and ascetic household in which he grew up, Rives becomes "aware not so much of inconveniences and privations of life at Good Range as of its moral compulsions." A burden seems "to have been laid upon all the members of his family to do good." [3]

In contrast to the idealism of the Georgia Allards, there are the Bradleys who own a general store in Clarksville. Belle Bradley is married to Jim Allard, grandson to Fontaine. Arthur Bradley, Belle's brother, later marries Love, a young woman who had been engaged to George Rowan. The Bradley's are opportunists somewhat like Faulkner's Snopeses. Their only guiding principle is money. They never take sides in the war, except to demand United States rather than Confederate currency from their customers.

In *None Shall Look Back*, there are, in effect, three heroes: Lucy Churchill, who is the technical hero of the novel; Rives Allard, who might be called the "code" hero; and Nathan Bedford Forrest, who is Miss Gordon's historical paradigm.[4] Lucy gives the novel its formal structure; for, though we see a good deal more of the war than Lucy does, the impact of the war is felt chiefly in the changes that take place in her. The other two heroes, though important, are integrated into the novel chiefly through their relationship with Lucy: Rives, because of his marriage to Lucy; Forrest, through his association with Rives.

Rives exemplifies in his conduct the kind of selflessness and fearlessness that many of Miss Gordon's fictional heroes display. He does not understand the arguments about politics, tariffs, and slavery—they merely confuse him. For him, the important fact is simply that "Our country had been invaded—it did not much matter on what grounds the invaders had come." [5] And so, though he has never thought about the war, or has never exulted in fighting as others had, when the time comes and men are needed for the defense of the country, Rives is glad to go. Throughout the rest of the novel, Rives displays the same uncomplicated devotion to duty that he was bred to at "Good Range." He is a soldier during the siege of Fort Donelson. When the fort is about to be surrendered to federal troops, he joins Forrest's rangers. Later, he goes on a spying mission for Forrest in the Yankee Army, a highly dangerous mission for which he gets neither acclaim nor promotion. When Rives is caught by the Yankees and is almost executed, he is saved only because the town in which he is being held prisoner is captured by Forrest.

After his rescue, Rives returns to his duties as one of Forrest's "orderlies." From this point on, the war goes from bad to worse. Rives is involved in conscripting unwilling men into Forrest's army; then he is shot in battle and is temporarily out of service. When he momentarily fears that the Southern cause is lost, he is depressed. Life for him would not be worth living if the South lost the war.[6] Later, when a guest at Brackets (his wife's home) suggests that Rives would have been better off if he had been permanently disabled and so out of the fighting, Rives grows angry and orders the man out of the house. His depression, anger, and the growing awareness of the South's plight only stiffen his resolve instead of defeating him. During a battle, which takes place near Franklin, Tennessee, the Confederate line wavers and breaks. General Forrest begs his men with tears in his eyes to rally, but they continue to fall back. Even the color bearer madly retreats. Rives's passion is aroused. He pursues the fleeing color bearer, shoots him, snatches up the banner, and carries it into the thick of the fighting. In the charge, he is wounded and falls dead from his horse.

III *The Soldier Hero*

In a novel by a writer with less talent and more infirm convictions than Caroline Gordon, Rives Allard might have remained little more than a sawdust hero doing copy-book deeds of valor. But Miss Gordon never falters in her vision of Rives as a man whose life has been one long preparation for doing his duty. She steadfastly avoids the labyrinth of his consciousness where the authors of antiheroes perfer to linger, and she shows us instead Rives Allard in action. This rendering of Allard's physical reality helps carry the conviction of the moral ideal of which he is also a symbol. Another important fictional technique for making Rives credible is Miss Gordon's use of Nathan Forrest as a heroic paradigm. Forrest "works" in a twofold manner: his personal example of selfless devotion to duty is a model and an inspiration to Rives; and he in part accounts for Rives's heroic actions, particularly in that last battle scene. But Forrest works on us as well, for whether we are inclined to value Forrest's kind of heroism, Forrest the man is beyond dispute. He was an actual person who did in fact the deeds ascribed to him. By making General Forrest a character in her novel, Miss Gordon not only adds the illusion of historical reality but also brings into the novel the code of conduct and attitude toward life by which these fictional realities are to be judged.

When Forrest appears very briefly in the early pages of the novel, he is simply a colonel who is recruiting young Kentuckians for his "rangers." In the opening chapters, the novel is dominated by the private lives of the Allard family; but as the narrative interest shifts more and more to the war, Forrest becomes increasingly important. We see him at Fort Donelson pleading unsuccessfully with his superiors not to surrender the fort, later at Nashville as he beats back a crowd of plundering soldiers, and at Chickamauga after the great Southern victory when he urges General Bragg unsuccessfully to pursue the retreating Union army. And we see that, though defeated by his superiors at the conference table, Forrest never really surrenders. When he is relieved of his command under Bragg, he persuades the Confederate government to allow him to raise his own army. We see him at the head of that army, a rag-tail outfit that continues to win victory after victory even while the other Confederate armies are beaten down by Union forces.

During most of the novel Bedford Forrest is presented, like Rives, from the outside; Forrest is a man of action. His deeds create him. But as the novel moves toward its close, the point of view moves closer to him; and we are permitted to hear what he hears and to see what he thinks. The most striking instance of this closer identification is in Chapter 1 of Book IV. The tale is almost done; the war, almost over; and Forrest himself is wounded on the sole of his foot and has been ordered to bed. In this chapter Miss Gordon has him recollect a battle he recently fought against General Sturgis. Instead of thinking the battle a useless expenditure of energy—for the war is all but lost—Forrest thinks of it rather as a "fight to hand down to your children and your children's children." [7] And the excitement of reliving that great battle gets Forrest out of bed against the doctor's orders and into the war again. Significantly, General Forrest is on hand when Rives Allard, bearing the colors he has just snatched from the hands of the retreating color bearer, dies in battle; and it is Forrest who catches up the colors and carries them toward the enemy.

Although it is by means of Rives and, especially Forrest, that Miss Gordon dramatizes the heroic virtues, she uses Lucy Churchill, the technical hero of the novel, to structure the action. The change in Lucy's fortune, the gradual movement from happiness to misery, constitutes the central structural principle. This movement begins on the first page, even before Lucy appears as a character; and the prevailing mood is happiness. A birthday celebration is going on for Fontaine Allard, Lucy's grandfather, who is sixty-five years old. But even in the midst of the celebration another mood is introduced, for the very name Fontaine, with its long vowel sounds, strikes a sad and ominous note in the opening sentence of the first chapter.

During Allard's birthday celebration, much of the talk is about the war that has just begun. The patriotic fervor, the excitement, and the sense of impending adventure have in the ears of the reader, who already knows the outcome, an ironic ring. Ironically, too, Lucy's personal happiness begins during this period of hectic excitement. And there is a foreshadowing of Lucy's fate in the fact that she spurns the young man who has been courting her and falls in love with her cousin Rives. The point is not that Lucy would have escaped her fate had she not married Rives; for George Rowan, her other suitor, is also killed in the war. The point is, rather, that the upheaval brings Lucy and Rives together and then, after they have loved, separates them. The love affair of Lucy and Rives is both a part of and a symbol of the fate of the society about which Miss Gordon is writing. We can see, moving to the allegorical level, that Lucy's choice of Rives is the one the South inevitably made when it took up arms—it shifted its trust from planters, like Fontaine Allard, to its citizen-soldiers,

like Forrest and Rives Allard. The South's fate, like Lucy's, is
already sealed.

IV   The Meaning of Slavery

An English critic, Walter Allen, has charged Miss Gordon with
ignoring the injustices of slavery in *None Shall Look Back* and of
writing, in effect, an apology for the old Southern way of life.[8]
It is true that Miss Gordon is not agonized by moral ambiguity
as is Faulkner, to whom Allen unfavorably compares her; but her
treatment of the Negro and of slavery is more complex than Allen
realizes. It should be pointed out that, though Miss Gordon has
some points in common with Faulkner, she is a different kind of
novelist. She is more detached, more contemplative, and more
Joycean in her refusal to allow her private emotions to show.
She takes the world—in this case—the Southern pre-Civil War
world—as she finds it, with its different classes, its different man-
ners, and its prejudices; out of these she constructs her drama.

I do not mean, as Allen suggests, that she whitewashes the
issue of slavery. In Chapter 6 (Part I) she dramatically presents
an instance of white brutality to a Negro slave. A white man, hired
by Fontaine Allard to oversee four hundred acres of land inherited
by Lucy from her mother, is discovered to have beaten the Negro
girl Della. The girl's wounds and suffering are graphically described, and Lucy is moved to pity for her and to outrage at the
way Della has been mistreated. But, at the same time, knowing
the girl very well and recalling the tricks that she often plays on
old Aunt Mimy, Lucy thinks that perhaps Della has provoked
the overseer beyond endurance. Lucy is confused and embarrassed
by these thoughts, just as anyone would be who responds to the
complexities of life rather than to theories about it.[9]

The incident of Della and the overseer is, like the war itself,
part of the enveloping action of Lucy's story. It brings dramatically
into the foreground one of the book's main themes—the inevitability
of suffering and human misery. At this point in the novel, Lucy,
moved by Della's suffering, is "ready to weep over the misery of
the world, but the next moment when she hears of a dance to be
held at the Rowan's, she is so happy that her heart almost bursts." [10]
This abrupt change in Lucy's mood will strike readers who prefer
moral tracts to fiction as inexplicable and callow. But, in Lucy,
Miss Gordon is depicting a normal young woman living in southern
Kentucky in the 1860's—one who, like normal young women every-

where, is usually at the mercy of her emotions. This change in
Lucy's mood foreshadows later and more permanent shifts from
happiness to misery and finally to despair. In this same chapter,
there are other hints at Lucy's tragic fate. There is some talk about
Lucy's getting married; and an old Negro woman, glancing slyly
at Rives, tells Lucy to be careful passing through the woods and
getting a crooked stick.[11] In marrying Rives, Lucy will not get a
crooked stick. Indeed, she will get a stick that is unusually straight
—so straight that it will finally be broken.

V *Lucy's Story*

The story of Lucy is interrupted for eight chapters while the
progress of the war is given. Fort Donelson has been surrendered
against the advice and pleading of Forrest; and the Yankees have
arrived at Clarksville, a town close to Brackets, the Allard's home.
In Chapter 10 (Part II), the scene shifts once more to the home
of Fontaine Allard; and we see the changes that have taken place.
The misery and the chaos hinted at in the beginning of the book
have deepened appreciably for the Allards. John McLean, Mrs.
Allard's half-brother, takes his money and departs for Canada. The
healthy Negroes run off, leaving Mrs. Allard to care not only for
her own family but also for the sick and aged Negroes. The mistress of the house is now the servant of servants. The overturning
of the old order is also dramatized at breakfast when Lucy's sister-
in-law Belle criticizes Fontaine Allard, and Allard actually "stoops"
to defend himself. Allard's stooping and later the sight of the confusion in the Negro quarters—the open cabin doors and the abandoned utensils and bedding—deepen Lucy's sadness. She thinks
of how "rats desert a sinking ship: 'We are sinking, sinking; and
they know it and have deserted us.'" [12]

At this point in the novel, the heroic qualities in Lucy's character
begin to appear; and they are brought out by the increasing misery
and suffering of the times, just as the war is to bring out the latent
heroism in Rives. When Ned, Lucy's brother, and Rives show up
at Brackets, having escaped from Fort Donelson with Forrest,
Lucy is filled with energy and purpose. She hustles about helping
everyone. Rives seems to her more assured in his bearing, and his
smile is so sweet when he asks her to go for a walk that she goes
promptly with him. The beginning of Lucy's serious love affair
with Rives coincides with the end of the way of life known to
and represented by her grandfather. The big house at Brackets is

burned to the ground by a careless Yankee soldier; Fontaine Allard
has a stroke from which he never recovers; and the family is forced
to move into a small house behind the big, burned one. Cally,
Lucy's aunt, a solid, practical, energetic woman bursts into tears.
Nobody knows how to do anything, she cries. There is "nobody
but me." [13] At this point, Lucy reveals that she and Rives are to
be married.

Aunt Cally, a solidly rendered minor character who is interesting
and convincing in her own right, is also used as a way of foreshadowing Lucy's fate. Cally too has been married, but her marriage turned out unhappily. When Lucy thinks of the failure of
Cally's marriage, she realizes "what a precarious business life—
and particularly love—is and how implacable the forces which
make for success or disaster. And it now seemed to her as im-
probable that she could be happy in this life as it had once seemed
certain." [14] Such insights do not, of course, keep Lucy from occasionally imagining that happiness is possible for herself. When
Rives takes her in his arms on his second visit to Brackets, Lucy
cries out, "Oh, I never thought I'd be happy again." [15] Her cry
of happiness is followed almost immediately by the arrival of the
Yankees at Brackets—the house is burnt, her grandfather is laid
low by a stroke, and capable Aunt Cally is reduced to helpless-
ness and tears.

Lucy's announcement of her engagement to Rives is not made
joyously. She is constrained and red-eyed when she breaks the
news to Aunt Cally. But yet there is a hopefulness implied in her
actions. Happiness is perhaps still possible. As the lovers, now
married, ride off to Rives's home, Miss Gordon evokes both the
intimate private world of the lovers and the doom that hangs
over them. The first sentence of the next chapter sounds an ominous note: "It was late in the afternoon." Rives and Lucy, riding
along a sandy road in north Georgia, pull up within sight of
Rives family's home. Rives points it out to her: "That black something there over the tallest pine. That's the house." [16] But Lucy
cannot see what he is pointing at. "The pines are so dark," she says.
"It makes the woods all look alike, Rives." The dark pine woods,
the gathering gloom, and the house itself, "a black oblong with
one murky light showing," give Lucy the fantastic notion that
Rives might have taken the wrong road.

There is a sinister fairy tale quality about this gloomy forest
and this journey. And Rives is like an innocent robber-bridegroom
leading Lucy to death. It is fitting that the lovers should arrive

just as darkness descends and that they should be greeted by the baying of the hounds and by the hooded figure of a woman standing in the doorway of Lucy's new home. Inside, in the firelight, the dark oblong of a house is more cheerful; but Lucy has been conducted into a marriage and into a life that is to be far different from what it might have been had there been no war. In the fairy tale, the bridgeroom turns out to be sinister; in Miss Gordon's novel, it is life itself.

The Allard house at "Good Range," though not unpleasant, is symbolic of the life Lucy is to lead. There is something bare and even grim about it. There are no carpets on the floor, and Lucy and Rives's bedroom looks more like a dormitory for boys than it does a lady's bedroom. Rives's sister and mother are different from the ladies at Brackets. Mitt, the sister, looks and acts like an old woman and Susan Allard, Rives's mother is somewhat mad. She has given away her china and furniture and even the dessert intended for her son and daughter-in-law's homecoming supper is sent to a dyspepsical neighbor. As an old Negro woman says of her, she goes "sashaying" around the countryside, and "half the time she don't know whar she gwine. She just gits on her horse and waits till the spirit move her." [17] Susan Allard is perhaps best understood as the author's way of particularizing the madness of the times and of suggesting that the possibility of happiness for Lucy is gone. The first night under her husband's roof, Lucy sees that Rives has his mother's eyes. Rives's madness, of course, is the madness of a hero, a man willing to fight and die for a cause—but that act lies still in the future. The next morning after their arrival, Rives takes Lucy out to see his land, and they inspect the site where they will build their house. The chapter ends with Lucy looking back and seeing their house there—"almost." [18]

VI *Lucy's Fate*

Part III of the novel begins with Rives in Chattanooga. Forrest is now a general, and Rives has been selected by a Sergeant Bigstaff to go on a spying mission among the Yankees. Back in Georgia Lucy receives a letter from Rives that recalls her memory of the last morning they had spent together in the woods at Good Range. Then there is, in flashback, a love scene that might have been presented directly at the time it occurred; but, on reflection, we recognize what is gained by this indirection: the pervading tone of *None Shall Look Back* is sadness, and to have presented the love affair directly in present time would have destroyed the tone. By presenting the scene in retrospect Miss Gordon is able to dramatize Lucy and Rives's passion while at the same time casting over it a sense of loss, almost of melancholy. At this point in the novel the two worlds—the public world of the battlefields and the private one of Lucy Allard—converge; and the reader is made to feel, through the private experience of Lucy, the whole weight of the coming catastrophe. The experience of Lucy is, in a sense, the Southern one. This is not to say that Miss Gordon is writing a historical allegory, but the stories of the war—the destruction of the South—and of the lovers parallel and reinforce each other.

But Lucy, like Rives, is still young and full of expectations. Defeat and bitterness are inconceivable to her—a fact nicely dramatized in Chapter 6 (Part III). As the chapter opens, Susan Allard is boiling castor beans. Her gray hair is askew; and beneath her faded calico blouse her homespun skirt sags; a strip of her flesh shows between. When the Negro woman Rivana ladles a little of the castor oil from the pot and invites Lucy to smell it, Lucy draws back, wrinkles her nose, and says, "I wouldn't take a dose of castor oil, if I were to die for it." Susan says, "Humph, you might be glad to get it, Miss."[19]

Lucy and Susan, of course, are talking about castor oil; but this action has a deeper significance. Before the chapter is over, Lucy has her first taste of death when a middle-aged Confederate captain is wounded in a skirmish and is carried in and placed in one of the Allards' beds. Lucy sits beside him holding his hand. When the captain dies, Mitty says, "We ought to shut his eyes." Lucy says, "I can't," but she does: She kneels down beside the bed and with her fingertips strokes the eye lids shut. After the captain's death, Lucy goes outside, crosses the porch, and feels in her bosom the sharp edge of Rives's letter, which has told her he cannot get a leave to come home. Lucy puts down her head and sobs. Susan appears and asks Lucy if the captain is dead. Lucy nods and Susan says, "Don't cry, he's better off." Lucy cries out loudly, "I'm not crying for him."[21] Rives and Lucy are to meet again before Rives's death, but in the death of this stranger Lucy has already experienced her lover's death.

VII   Heroes and Nonheroes

The next seven chapters of Part III (8–14) deal mainly with the war—the bloody battle of Chickamauga that results in a vic-

tory for the South and in death for Lucy's old suitor George
Rowan and Rives's comrade, Sergeant Bigstaff. Rives survives
this battle and attends Forrest on a wild ride to the headquarters
of General Bragg, commander of the Confererate forces. Forrest
wants to pursue the Yankees; Bragg refuses. Rives, who overhears
their conversation, thinks that life will not be worth living if the
Confederate cause is lost. The meeting between Bragg and Forrest
and Rives's comment on the war foreshadow the coming end.
Bragg, "the man with the iron hand, the iron heart and the wooden
head,"[22] cares more for his own personal glory than for winning
battles. It is said that he refuses to pursue the Yankees after the
stunning defeat at Chickamauga because he wants to ride into
Chattanooga the next morning as the conquering hero.[23] This
characterization of Bragg (which, by the way, shows that Miss
Gordon is not merely writing a defense of the ante-bellum South,
as some critics believe) is also a way of underscoring Forrest's
virtues. Bragg is not a hero, he is not a selfless man devoted to
causes.

There are also several fictional characters whose concern is for
themselves alone: Joe Bradley, a shrewd storekeeper, takes no
sides in the war; for his only concern is to make money. Early in
the war he prudently puts his money in United States bonds; and
then, seeing that the war is going against the South, he accepts
only United States currency from his customers. Jim, Lucy's
brother who is married to Joe Bradley's daughter and who is perhaps the archvillain of the novel, shares Bradley's view of the
war. When Jim's younger brother Ned comes home sick and
broken from a Yankee prison camp, Jim is repelled by Ned's appearance and thinks it would be just as well if Ned died. When
Ned talks about re-enlisting, Jim tells him not to be foolish; the
South is going to lose the war. Later, when Ned talks about going
back to Brackets to farm, Jim tells him there is nothing in farming; the store, Jim contends, is the place to be because it is the
only place where money can be made.

There is one Allard woman who sells out: Love, who becomes
engaged to George Rowan after Lucy refuses him. After Rowan's
death at Chickamauga, Love becomes engaged to Arthur Bradley,
Joe Bradley's son, who did not serve in the war. When Love announces her engagement, Aunt Cally is outraged; but Love de-
fensively replies that she now loves Arthur more than George.
Cally then makes a comment that summarizes one side of the
novel's moral vision: "There's just two kind of people in the

world, those that'll fight for what they think right and those that don't think anything is worth fighting for."[24] The best people in *None Shall Look Back* are always capable of devoting themselves to something outside of themselves—to the land, to their families, to their region. The worst people are those without feeling except for themselves and their own personal advancement. Either they care for nothing but money, like the Bradleys, or they are concerned, like Bragg, with the figure they cut in the world.

Lucy, of course, must be numbered among the best people. When Rives comes home wounded and dejected and fails to respond to her and when at night his face in repose looks like marble, Lucy is upset and frightened. When Rives rides back to the front—still cold and emotionless—Lucy cries. Unlike Love, however, she is not fickle; she continues to love Rives no matter what happens. The novel ends shortly after Rives's death in battle. Forrest lives to carry on the fight, but Lucy, the technical hero of the novel, looks out at a world that has now altered; "She watched the light go from the sky and knew that when she saw the green fields of Kentucky again they would be as alien as the gullied, pine-clad slopes outside the window."[25]

VIII *Universal Implications*

There is little reason to doubt that the loss of the Civil War by the South was for Caroline Gordon, as for many Southerners, a hauntingly sad defeat. It is possible to imagine her as the prototype of a young Southern woman in *Penhally* who found a long, ill-written poem about the Civil War in a Paris bookstall and, despite its crudeness, was reduced to tears by it. *None Shall Look Back* reflects the haunting sorrow of the South's fate, but it does so through the lives of two fictional characters, Lucy and Rives Allard. And so, because the sadness is objectified in the lives of these characters, it never becomes sentimental. Indeed, the story of Lucy's loss becomes a universal one about human loss and suffering.

Death and suffering, loss of love and loss of life—these are the inevitable lot of man: "Stand, stand, shall they cry; but none shall look back."[26] All that makes having lived count is the having stood—of having committed oneself in word and in deed to another person, to a higher cause, to something outside oneself. The standing, the commitment, has nothing to do with personal survival. Like Forrest's "useless" battle, the commitment is a legacy to be handed down to one's children.

CHAPTER 6

An Agrarian Hero

THE year 1937 was a productive one for Caroline Gordon. Early in that year she published *None Shall Look Back* and a few months later *The Garden of Adonis*, both fairly long and complex works.[1] It is interesting that although these books were written close together, they are, on the face of it, rather different kinds of novels. *None Shall Look Back* is in large part "researched," for it is set in the past, and its protagonist is more or less conventionally heroic. *The Garden of Adonis*, on the contrary, is about the contemporary world: the drought-stricken depression years of the 1930's, and the hero is a farmer who is killed in an apparently futile attempt to keep a field of clover from being destroyed. Despite some very real differences, both novels relate essentially the same story Miss Gordon tells in *Penhally* and will tell again in other novels—the stand and fall of an ordinary person who is extraordinarily heroic. What is really unusual about *The Garden of Adonis* is that Miss Gordon does not depend as she had in her other novels on factual history and historical paradigm; instead, she uses a mythical one, a technique probably suggested by T. S. Eliot's long poem *The Waste Land*.

Instead of employing the maimed hero as her prototype, however, Miss Gordon invokes the ancient Adonis myth, taking as the epigraph for *The Garden of Adonis* a quotation from Sir James Frazer's *The Golden Bough*. The epigraph describes the spring ritual practiced in Western Asia and in Greek lands in ancient times of making "gardens of Adonis, which were baskets or pots filled with earth, in which wheat, barley, lettuces, fennel and various kinds of flowers were sown and tended for eight days, chiefly or exclusively by women. Fostered by the sun's heat, the plants shot up rapidly, but having no root they withered as rapidly away, and at the end of eight days were carried out with the images of the dead Adonis, and flung with them into the sea or into springs."[2] The purpose of this ritual, Frazer explains, was to promote the growth or revival of vegetation. In very early times "Adonis was sometimes impersonated by a living man who died a violent death in the character of the god" and sometimes "by human victims slain on the harvestfield." The purpose of these ritual murders were to propitiate the corn spirit in the belief that the spirits of the victims would return to live in the ears of corn fattened by their blood.[3]

I   *The Myth and the Story*

While it is not essential that the reader be familiar with the myth of Adonis in order to understand *The Garden of Adonis*, such knowledge helps us see what Miss Gordon was attempting in this novel. Her Adonis is a Tennessee planter named Ben Allard; and, like other of Miss Gordon's heroes, Allard loves the soil above all else; and as a result, his constant concern is to make the crops that he and his tenants plant thrive. But Allard works under terrible handicaps: his land has suffered a drought for two years; the bankers who hold a mortgage on his plantation will not extend him credit; his tenants are a shiftless, careless lot—except for the Mortimers, who resemble Allard in his devotion to the soil.

In the Mortimer family there is the father, old Joe, who is seventy years old, and his wife Nora and their son Ote, aged twenty-four, who has just returned from a three-year stay in Detroit. The Mortimers are self-sufficient, hard-working, decent farmers; but they are also stubborn and somewhat difficult to manage. Allard's other tenants are the Sheelers, shiftless, no-account people with "nasty" ways. Ironically, Ote Mortimer falls in love with one of the Sheeler girls, Idelle; and this love affair eventually precipitates the tragic conclusion of the novel in which Ote Mortimer kills Ben Allard.

The novel begins with the arrival of the Mortimer family on Allard's farm, and the point of view shifts almost immediately to the son Ote, who is one of the major characters in the novel. In this first chapter, Ote's murder of Allard is foreshadowed by a dream in which Ote sees himself lying dead in his coffin. In the second chapter, Allard is introduced; and the conflict that is to arise between him and Ote is established. When Allard suggests that, instead of planting alfalfa, they plant a new kind of clover called "Lespedeza," Joe Mortimer immediately gets a stubborn look on his face; and Allard feels an immense weariness descend upon him as he thinks of all of the thousands of veiled and stubborn eyes, like those of Joe Mortimer, that he has looked into. Such people were "like dumb, driven cattle" who "were so mortally afraid of being driven they would do *anything* to bring your efforts to naught. . . ."[4] Allard foresees the time when he will grow so weary of such tenants that he will lie down and let them shovel him under. Although Ote's father refuses to plant the new type of clover, Ote readily agrees to do so. Ironically, this field planted with Lespedeza brings about the fatal conflict between Ben Allard and Ote Mortimer.

Allard also plants tobacco "on shares" with the Mortimers, but the drought ruins the entire crop. Only the field planted with hay and Lespedeza does well. In the normal course of events, these crops would have grown to maturity and would have been cut; but Ote's affair with Idella takes a turn that makes Ote desperate for money: Idelle is pregnant and wants Ote to marry her. In his desperation, Ote turns to the only source available—to the field which he and Allard have planted on shares. Although Allard advises Ote that the hay in the field cannot be mowed without ruining the Lespedeza planted with it and warns him to stay out of the field, Ote, when he learns that Idelle has run off to marry his rival, Buck Chester, hitches up the mower and drives it furiously into the field. Allard tries to stop him by standing in the path of the mower, but Ote jumps down, picks up a singletree and strikes Allard dead.

Although Ote Mortimer kills Ben Allard, we can see that he is only the instrument of Allard's destruction. He acts, symbolically, for the culture and the society within which Allard lives—a culture and a society basically hostile to the agrarian values that Allard represents. And this is another basic difference between the culture that produced the Adonis myth and the one that destroys Ben Allard. This contrast, suggested by the epigraph from *The Golden Bough,* is Miss Gordon's way of underscoring her meaning and of giving authority to her point of view. This contrast also provides a clue, if one is needed, for reading the novel in the right perspective.

II   *The Town versus the Country*

In addition to the country people—Ben Allard, the Mortimers, the Sheelers—there are also a number of town people (among whom must be counted Allard's son and daughter) whose basic values and way of life are antagonistic to and destructive of the agrarian values represented by Allard. It is these town people in whose name Ote symbolically acts. In a sense, the rest of the novel is devoted to creating characters and actions which dramatize that antagonistic culture and makes us feel its destructiveness.

Among these town characters are two important families, the Carters and the Camps. The Carters, an old Alabama family, were once farmers; they now live in a halfway world between the town and country, just outside of Countsville, Alabama. Carter, the father, was born on the farm; but he gave up farm life to study law. He died at his desk in town of a heart attack at an early age, leaving his widow and seven children. Members of the Carter family who figure prominently in this story are the son Jim, his sister Helen, and their mother. Jim Carter, being the youngest son of an impoverished family, is unable to go to college. He has a genuine talent for raising dogs; but, at his mother's insistence, he gives up his dogs to go to Saint Louis to work at insurance advertising. Eight years later, he returns to Countsville to take over the local office of the insurance firm. Helen Carter, his sister, is important principally because it is through her that the Carters are brought into relationship with the Camp family.

The Camps, whose name was originally Kampschafer, had come to Alabama from New Jersey, bringing with them a business that manufacturers baby diapers and a product called simply "fascinex." The Camp family consists of the father, a small, white-haired, "cultured" man and the mother, a small white-haired woman who thinks that money grows on trees and who sees her children through "rose-colored glasses." The children, Joe and Sara, have been to "the best" Eastern schools, have traveled widely, and have been allowed to have pretty much what they wanted—including an elaborate swimming pool with a guest house that has a bar and a Jamaican Negro in attendance.

The Camps and the younger Carters represent a way of life diametrically opposed to the principles embodied by Ben Allard. Like the modern Nicholas Llewellyn of *Penhally*, the Camps and Carters have no strong attachments except to money. Helen Carter deliberately pursues and marries Joe Camp because he is rich. Their elaborate wedding is paid for by Camp money. Jim Carter, who has a little more principle than his sister, elopes with Sara Camp after a drunken party. The Carters, the Camps, and the money culture they represent are brought in conflict with the agrarian world of Ben Allard through Allard's daughter Letty and his son Frank. Like his friend Jim Carter, Frank Allard has left the country to go to work in town for an insurance concern; and his sister Letty, bored with country life, leaves her father's farm whenever she can to visit her brother in Countsville. There she meets Jim Carter at a time when he has quarreled with and separated from Sara. Letty pursues Carter, who first resists but later succumbs to her charms.

III The Structure and Meaning

The setting up and working out of the relationships between various pairs of young men and women constitute a good portion of the novel. The meaning of those relationships, however, is suggested by a number of important parallels. As we have noted, Helen Carter pursues and marries Joe Camp because of his money; Jim Carter marries Sara Camp when he is drunk because he senses that she feels "insecure" and requires his social position.[5] Carter also has a rather protracted affair with a prostitute in Countsville named Babe Worsham. Because of boredom, Letty Allard pursues Jim Carter and invites him to seduce her. The love affairs, if I may call them that, are a tepid combination of lust, convenience, and greed in which the women are the aggressors and the men are little more than passive victims.

Miss Gordon's way of commenting on the lives of these young townspeople is to contrast them to two genuine love affairs; those of Ote Mortimer and Idelle Sheeler and, by means of flashback, of Ben Allard and Maggie Carew. Ote's love for Idelle, though misplaced—for Idelle's principles are not much higher than those of prostitute Babe Worsham—is at least a genuine passion. He does the pursuing; and, in order to win Idelle's favor, he has to "take her away" from a bootlegger named Buck Chester. Ote is so passionately attracted to Idelle that he is driven into a mad fury when he finally loses her. In contrast to Ote, Jim Carter cares almost nothing for Sara Camp. His most passionate affair is with Babe Worsham, and he is rather easily seduced by Letty Allard.

The most telling comment on the young people in this novel, however, is made by the contrast with the love of Ben Allard for Maggie Carew. Allard had loved Maggie for something like ten years and had planned to marry her, but he caught her one day in the embrace of another man. Maggie tried to smooth things over with Allard: "She had cried and talked a lot. He hardly listened. When she stopped he shook his head. 'It's no use, Maggie. It's like you were dead. You are—to me'."[6] Ben Allard was only a boy at the time, but from then on, he rarely allowed his mind to dwell upon either Maggie Carew or Ed Ruffin, her lover. "There had been times when his effort not to think of them had been actual physical pain: a dull ache in the head that went on night after night. Or it had been like tearing out a piece of flesh—for he had been in love with Maggie Carew...."[7]

Miss Gordon does not explicitly make the connection to the pairs of lovers, but the reader can only interpret this scene in the light of all the tepid affairs that have gone before. Moreover, as Allard recalls his love for Maggie Carew, Jim Carter, his son's friend, whom he trusts as a man of honor, is preparing to seduce his daughter in Allard's own house. The juxtaposition of Allard's response to his fiancée's infidelity with Carter's shameless betrayal of his host's trust is the author's way of suggesting an essential difference between Allard's world and that of the Carters and Camps.

It is also significant that Carter's betrayal of Ben Allard's trust and Letty's flight from her father's house occur shortly before Allard is murdered by Ote Mortimer. Indeed, because Allard is upset about his domestic difficulties, he speaks sharply to Ote when warning him to stay out of the field of Lespedeza. And Ote's troubles with his woman and his shortage of money, as well as his conflict with Allard, precipitate his violence. In that final scene, then, everything comes to focus; and the loss of the field becomes an objective correlative for the loss of all that Ben Allard stands for. It also makes us aware of him as the victim of a sacrifice that is meaningless to everyone but him. But, whether the world recognizes it or not, Ben Allard is a hero; he is a man who stands for what he believes, even to the point of giving up his life. For Miss Gordon, there is meaning not only in that act but in what the act stands for—the concept of life that made it possible.

IV *Universal Implications*

Although the use of the mythical paradigm employed in *The Garden of Adonis* is, on the face of it, a technique different from anything Miss Gordon had used before, in principle it is significantly like the historical paradigm. For considered in perspective, the mythical paradigm is simply the historical paradigm pushed back in time. To be sure, the Adonis myth would not have for modern readers the kind of authority that the life of Nathan

Bedford Forrest could; but it is more flexible, and, if skillfully used, is convincing in its own way, through the authority lent the writer in both the conception and creation of the fictional model of the paradigm. The important thing, in other words, is that the writer be convinced and that this conviction be communicated to the reader through tone rather than through attempts to provide numerous realistic parallels to the myth.

To be sure, explicit references to Adonis in the title and in the epigraph are ways of calling the reader's attention to the parallel and of inviting him to see what the novel very indirectly suggests: that, though the killing of Ben Allard was precipitated by events that occurred during the 1930's in Tennessee and Alabama, it was also a timeless story about the conflict between the creative and the destructive sides of man. To put this another way, Miss Gordon seems to suggest that the death of Ben Allard, which is in part caused by the drought and the depression, could not have been prevented by man-made remedies as some novels in the 1930's were suggesting.[8] Times and conditions may change, but man does not. And man, or the destructive element in him, is responsible for the killing of heroes like Ben Allard.

CHAPTER 7

A Pioneer Hero

Four years passed between the publication in 1937 of *The Garden of Adonis* and the appearance in 1941 of *Green Centuries*, Caroline Gordon's next book. *Green Centuries* is a long historical novel about life on the Kentucky frontier around the time of the American Revolution, and we can see from the abundance of concrete detail that Miss Gordon spent a great deal of time reading historical material and studying the territory she was to write about. However, *Green Centuries* is not an ordinary historical novel, for the researched material is perfectly assimilated and subordinated to the fiction. Indeed, there is about this novel a freshness and sense of what Henry James called "felt life";[1] and, we feel, as we must in a historical novel if it is to be convincing, that "it must have happened just this way."

In large part, Miss Gordon's use of accurate historical detail helps produce this effect: her inclusion of the names of actual persons, Indian and white; the use of specific towns and villages; and references to historical events such as the signing of a treaty by the Cherokee Indians transferring the vast tract of Kentucky to the white man Richard Henderson. The meticulous attention to details of dress, travel, warfare, woodcraft, and husbandry also help convince us that these characters must have lived and that these events have happened just as the author has recorded them. The truth is, of course, that Miss Gordon has carefully selected and arranged her material in order to make us see it in the light of her own special apprehension.

In addition to factual historical material, including the use of a famous historical figure, Miss Gordon again employs a mythical paradigm; but it is so lightly emphasized that few readers would consciously make the connection between the protagonist of this novel, Rion Outlaw, and the paradigmatic hero, Orion, of Greek myth. And yet the Orion myth works here in the same way that the Adonis myth does in *The Garden of Adonis*. It underscores the universal implications of the novel; but, more important, it permeates the novel, elevates the tone, and consequently lifts the story Miss Gordon tells above its solid base of historical fact and realistic detail.

I   *The Myth and the Story*

The historical paradigm of *Green Centuries* is Daniel Boone, who also resembles the mythical paradigm, Orion, the giant hunter who pursued the bull but never made the kill and who, after his death, was placed among the stars. Both historical and mythical paradigms are introduced early in the novel: Orion merely through a reference to the Greek myth, and Boone through his introduction as a fictional character. Both paradigms, significantly, are brought together in the same scene. Rion Outlaw, protagonist of *Green Centuries,* who is waiting outside of Daniel Boone's cabin, looks up at Orion in the sky and feels that he, Rion Outlaw, is the mighty hunter come down to earth. Rion hopes to accompany Boone on an expedition into the vast wilderness of Kentucky. "I'll hunt over that meadow," he cries.[2]

In a sense, *Green Centuries* is the account of Rion Outlaw's living out of that boast. He never actually hunts across Kentucky, and he forgets his kinship with Orion until the close of the novel. However, the whole impulse of his life is to push on into the West, to encounter hardships and dangers, and to take these in his stride. Rion becomes an outlaw when he helps blow up a powder train being sent to reinforce the British garrison at Hillsborough. Later he leads a small band of outlaws across the hazardous Blue Ridge Mountains, bargains with the Cherokees for land, helps defend a stockade against Indian attacks, loses his children in an Indian raid, and finally is deprived of his wife. It is only the death of his wife, Cassie, that makes Rion aware of how he has "lost himself in the turning."

At the close of the novel, when the name of the mythical Orion is again invoked, the reader is invited to see how Rion Outlaw, an American pioneer, has in his own unselfconscious way come about as close to achieving human greatness as a mere mortal can. If Rion is not lifted up into the stars as was his prototype, he is elevated by Miss Gordon's tone:

When he was a boy on the Yadkin he used to like to think that he took his name from the mighty hunter, and out in the woods at night or coming home from a frolic he would look up and pick out the

stars: the hunter's foot, his club, his girdle, the red eye of the bull
that he pursued ever westward . . . His father had come west across
the ocean, leaving all that he cared about behind. And he himself as
soon as he had grown to manhood had looked at the mountains and
could not rest until he knew what lay beyond them. But it seemed
that a man had to flee farther each time and leave more behind him
and when he got to the new place he looked up and saw Orion fixed
upon his burning wheel, always pursuing the bull but never making the
kill. Did Orion will any longer the westward chase? No more than
himself. Like the mighty hunter he had lost himself in the turning.[3]

Although Rion Outlaw is the technical hero of the novel, another
character embodies some of the same heroic qualities but in a
simpler more primitive form: the Indian chief Dragging Canoe.
Dragging Canoe, who is about the age of Rion, is reputed to be
the strongest man in the Cherokee Nation: "Once when the river
was in flood he had swum across it three times, rescuing children
and women who were too old to swim."[4] In the ordinary historical
novel the Indian chief would be cast as the villain; or perhaps, in
a more "enlightened" book, he would be the real hero and his white
opponent the villain. Miss Gordon, however, does not resort to such
simple moral stances. For her, the distinguishing quality of the
hero is his determination to stand up for principles, his people,
his way of life. And so, though Dragging Canoe inevitably becomes
Rion Outlaw's antagonist because fate has pitted them against each
other, they are essentially alike, fearlessly devoted to their own
way of life.

Dragging Canoe is the only Indian chief strong enough and determined enough to stand up against the white settlers. His father,
Atta Kulla Kulla, has been to England and knows that the white
man's "medicine" is invincible; but Dragging Canoe, who has never
been out of Indian territory, knows only that he will never surrender
to the white man. Atta Kulla Kulla prefers to trade land to the
whites in hopes of avoiding war, but Dragging Canoe would rather
fight than sell out. For a time, Atta Kulla Kulla's advice holds sway:
the Cherokees appease the white man by trading him, piece by
piece, Indian land. But Dragging Canoe finally prevails; he leads
his people into a war in which defeat of the Indian forces is certain.

Miss Gordon shows us that Dragging Canoe's tragic greatness lies
in his refusal to surrender. Some readers have been disturbed by
Miss Gordon's apparent refusal to take sides in the struggle between
Indian and whites; others evidently believe her more sympathetic to
the Indians than to her white protagonist. But the truth is that Miss

Gordon's sympathies are not distributed on the basis of color or race. If the Indians are more sympathetically presented, that may be because they most fully embody qualites that Miss Gordon admires —the willingness to stand on principle. The certain defeat of the Indian forces makes their heroism all the more poignant.

II   *Conclusion*

One of the most interesting and also one of the most ambiguous sections of the novel deals with the life of Rion's younger brother Archie Outlaw, who is taken captive by the Indians, adopted into the tribe, married to an Indian girl, and later killed in an Indian village when it is destroyed by white settlers, among whom is Rion Outlaw himself. The sections of the novel dealing with Archie's life among the Indians are as well written and convincing as the chapters about the white settlers. Archie functions as a transition or bridge between the two cultures. Through him and his friendly relations to Indians and whites, Miss Gordon suggests the essential humanity of both Indian and white and makes us feel the justness with which each side views its own actions.

There is ambiguity, however, in how the reader is to respond to Archie himself. He seems to adjust too easily to Indian life, for he not only adopts Indian ways but even scalps white settlers. When Rion gives Archie the opportunity to escape from his captors, Archie chooses to remain among the Indians. If we applied Miss Gordon's implicit definition of heroism, we might conclude that Archie is a traitor to his own people, for he has, in a sense, sold out. But Archie's youth is on his side, for he was fairly young when taken captive, and he does develop into a fearless brave. Toward the end of the novel, when the main Indian forces have been defeated, he stands by Dragging Canoe and pleads for an important assignment as a messenger to the British general. However, this ambiguity, this refusal to make a clear-cut judgment about Archie, makes him an interesting and complicated character.

It is Rion and, above all, Dragging Canoe who dominate the novel. Clearly, Miss Gordon's imagination was deeply involved in the creation of these two characters. She was able to see them, create them in all the illusion of their physical reality, but at the same time shape them to the bent of her own heroic vision. There is no editorializing, no simple illustration of moral conduct. The only explicit statement she permits herself is a brief quotation from a letter Gustave Flaubert wrote Louise Colet which stands as the epigraph to Part IV of the novel. Since it is brief and nicely sums up Miss Gordon's own response to the heroic characters in this novel, it is worth quoting: "I have in me the melancholy of the barbaric races with their migratory instincts and inborn tastes for a life that makes them leave their country rather than change themselves".[5]

The futile struggle of a single powerful individual who is determined to fight on for the things his society has already surrendered produces the melancholy ending of *Green Centuries*. The struggle is admirable, the inevitable defeat, sad. This same mixture of admiration and melancholy is reflected in the conclusion of a number of Caroline Gordon's novels, such as *Penhally, None Shall Look Back*, and *The Garden of Adonis*.

Green Centuries is the kind of novel that literary analysis cannot do justice to. It is intellectually uncomplicated, but it works powerfully on the emotions. Moreover, it comes closer to achieving Miss Gordon's idea of a purely dramatic fiction than any of the other novels. What is said and the manner of the saying are so closely related that it is almost impossible to discuss the novel in the abstract. To say so is to pay it high tribute.

CHAPTER 8

The Hero in the Modern World

In her critical work *How to Read a Novel*, Caroline Gordon makes it clear that she sees no reason why the hero of a modern novel should be essentially different from the hero of a Greek tragedy or of an eighteenth-century English novel.[1] A hero is a man who "overcomes evil that good may flourish."[2] Such statements, however, are a declaration of faith rather than a description of what Miss Gordon has found to be true in a good many modern novels. Indeed, as we have seen, Miss Gordon maintains that the protagonists of writers like André Gide and Jean Paul Sartre are not heroes at all, for they are incapable of acting.[3] The protagonists of Miss Gordon's own novels, of course, do resemble the traditional hero she describes; but, as we have also seen, these heroes inevitably do not come from the modern world but from cultures of the past. Furthermore, two of Miss Gordon's novels have shown the modern world to be deeply hostile to the concept of heroism that she holds to be timeless, which is not to say that she contradicts herself but only that she herself has had difficulty creating in a wholly contemporary setting the kind of heroes she admires. And this problem is inevitable, for any novelist who is widely read in modern literature and who is aware of the current state of intellectual thought is bound to be influenced by the current attraction to the introverted, paralyzed hero, a protagonist Miss Gordon scornfully rejects.

Obviously, it is easier to say that true heroes are essentially the same in all ages than it is to create convincing traditional heroes in an age that no longer believes in them. If a novelist writes about his own time, he writes in the shadow of the myths of his time, whether he wishes to or not; and the myths necessarily include concepts of the hero that the writer must come to terms with. As we have seen, Miss Gordon solved the dilemma simply by avoiding it, by writing about a world with myths different from those of her own time. But in her sixth novel, *The Women on the Porch* (1944), Caroline Gordon was ready to deal with the modern hero, the paralyzed intellectual, not because she had renounced her belief in the traditional hero, but because she had devised a way of having him escape the labyrinths of his tormented mind, reside in the world of flesh and blood, and assume ordinary human responsibilities. Even the paralyzed hero, then, would fit the definition of the traditional hero if he could be made to act in a meaningful way.

I *The Story and the Symbols*

On the literal level, *The Women on the Porch* might be read as the story of a marriage that has gone wrong. Catherine Chapman, a thirty-five-year-old woman, suddenly discovers that her husband, Jim Chapman, a brilliant scholar and professor of history, has been having an affair with his young assistant, Edith Ross. Catherine hurriedly packs her suitcase, takes her dog, and leaves New York for Swan Quarter, Tennessee, where her grandmother, her Aunt Daphne, and her cousin Willy still live on the land settled by their pioneer forebears. Presently, Catherine, shocked and hurt by her husband's infidelity, allows herself to be drawn into an affair with a cousin, Tom Manigault, who lives on an adjoining farm with his mother Elsie Manigault and a visiting New York architect, Roy Miller. Back in New York, Jim Chapman comes to realize that he does not love Edith Ross. Without his wife, Catherine, life is futile and meaningless. He takes the train to Swan Quarter; and after an emotional bout with Catherine in which her affair with Tom Manigault is exposed, a reconciliation is effected. The novel ends with Jim Chapman's stooping to replace a slipper on his wife's foot: While "still holding it in his hand, he bent lower and set his lips on her bare instep."[4]

In summary, *The Women on the Porch* sounds quite different from the kind of novel it actually is; for it is neither a love story nor a domestic tragedy. The relationship of Catherine and Tom Manigault is treated indirectly. There is only one scene in which the lovers embrace; the beginning, the early stages in the development of the affair, and Tom's dismissal are simply alluded to. The relationship of Catherine and Jim is more fully developed, but it is presented mainly through flashbacks. The reconciliation at Swan Quarter takes place in the space of less than six pages, and there is little psychological or emotional analysis of Catherine or Jim Chapman. The point is not that Miss Gordon has failed to do her job properly, for her interest is less in the social or physical texture of her characters' lives and much more in what these lives can be made to suggest. If *Women on the Porch* lacks the density of surface texture that novels such as Tolstoi's *Anna Karenina* and Flaubert's *Madame Bovary* have, it has instead the suggestiveness of James's *Portrait of a Lady*. And the reason, of course, is that, like James, Miss Gordon's interest in her materials, despite a seeming preoccupation with surfaces, is ultimately in the moral implications of her narrative.

Yet the literal level of objects and physical beings and ordinary actions, though a means to an end, is as always, firmly there. As the novel opens, two Tennessee countrymen are seated on the gallery of a run-down country store and gasoline station near Swan Quarter, which is to be the setting of much of the action of the novel. Suddenly they hear the sound of a motor. As they look up toward a distant hill, a speeding car appears. It moves on down the road, appearing and disappearing behind trees and shrubbery; and it finally stops beside the gasoline pump. The driver, a young woman, leans out and says, "Fill her up, please." It is Catherine Chapman, and her voice is "as dry as the dust that lay thick on her face, her hands, her long, light brown hair."[5] The dust, like the car with its New York license plate, the dog named Heros—indeed, the flight of Catherine herself—are all symbolic.

What the symbolism points to becomes increasingly clear as the action of the novel moves forward. Swan Quarter, which was built by Catherine's pioneer forebears and to which she is now fleeing in her time of unhappiness, turns out to be an isolated place shut off from the outside road by a thicket of bushes, vines, and saplings. Catherine fights her way through the thicket and arrives, her stockings torn and her legs bleeding from the brambles, on the lawn of the "gray spreading bulk of the house." On the porch of the house sit three women. For a moment it seems to Catherine: "that she had never seen these women before; and then she knew them for her aunt, her grandmother and her cousin and she called out their names and ran toward them."[6] The three women are like the three fates; and, in running toward them, Catherine in a sense runs to meet her doom; for the three women in their different ways represent living death.

The grandmother is so old and senile that she has to be cared for like a child, but she manages to keep the other women in the house under her control. Toward the close of the novel, she suffers a stroke that separates her completely from the life around her. She

recovers physically, but mentally lives during Civil war times; and
she addresses her daughter and niece by names of long-since dead
relatives. The niece, Catherine Chapman's Aunt Daphne, is a tire-
some old maid whose chief interest in life (or death, it might better
be called) is in collecting, classifying, and in eating mushrooms.
Among her favorite specimens is the one *Trompette du Mort*.
Daphne's preoccupation with mycology, as she calls it, aptly
symbolizes the life-in-death quality of her life. Catherine's cousin
Willy, the third woman on the porch, is a more lively and also a
more complex character than Daphne. Like Daphne. Willy is un-
married; but she is not, like Daphne, unmarriageable. But Willy has
devoted herself to the care and support of her mother and her
aunt. She runs the farm, or tries to, and makes a bad job of it.

II   *Structure and Meaning*

Cousin Willy's "meaning" is crucial to the novel, for it is principally through her that Miss Gordon comments symbolically on
Catherine and on her relationship with her husband. Cousin Willy
has come into possession of a fine chestnut-colored stallion, the
Tennessee walking horse named Red. When she is persuaded
partly by Catherine and partly by her tenant and manager, Mr.
Shannon, to exhibit Red at the county fair, Red takes first prize;
and Willy has dreams of breeding Red and raising colts. "Red
Allen, by Roan Allen out of Miss Fancy. At stud," she thinks.
"Twenty-five dollars."[7]
Miss Gordon makes no explicit moral judgment about Willy's
ambition, but it is clear that, like the other two women on the
porch, Willy is living a kind of underworld existence. She rejects
the honorable proposal of marriage offered her by Mr. Shannon;
she refuses an offer of $10,000 for Red, and she decides, instead, to
carry him off to another horse show. Red, however, does not survive
the first showing at the county fair; and his destruction puts the
final cap of meaning on Willy's actions. The death of Red occurs
because of loose boards on his stall at the Fairgrounds and a naked
electric light bulb that hangs outside the stall. Willy sees the loose
boards; but being a woman who knows less about horses and car-
pentry than she should, she merely pushes Red's head back through
the opening, saying. "Bad boy . . . you're a bad boy."[8] Mr. Shannon,
who is taking his orders from Willy, looks about for a tool; and,
when he can't find one, he slips the board back in place and ham-
mers it with his fist. "I'll have that fixed tomorrow," he says.[9] But

tomorrow is too late, for that night, Red pushes through the boards again, chomps just once on the electric light bulb, and is electrocuted.

The horse Red provides the most important symbol in the novel. Shortly after she arrives at Swan Quarter, Catherine discovers Red and insists on riding him. News of Red's death, along with the return of Willy to Swan Quarter, coincides with the reconciliation of Tom and Catherine Chapman. On the level of allegory, Red stands for brute primitive force. In her possession of Red, Willy (the masculine name, a shortened form of Wilhelmina) has attempted to fill the role normally filled by a man. Her spinsterhood, her refusal of Mr. Shannon, and her dream of conducting a stud service symbolize Willy's attempt to avoid the woman's role assigned her by fate. Readers who take what is called "an enlightened view" of the role of women may raise objections to this reading, but Miss Gordon here and in other places makes it plain that woman's proper role is to serve and to follow. When woman attempts to lead and direct, the moral order is disrupted and disaster ensues.[10]

This point is more fully devloped in the sections of the novel dealing with the Manigault family. Elsie Manigault, an Eastern woman, married Edward Manigault whose family originally owned the farm that Elsie and her son Tom now own jointly. Edward Manigault left the farm and went East to practice law. Tom was reared in New York, but he returned to Tennessee to live the life of a farmer. He is a kind of throwback to his rural ancestors, a "natural man," as someone in the novel calls him.[11] Tom's mother, a "cultured," well-cared-for beauty, has followed Tom to Tennessee, mainly because she cannot stand Tom's being independent of her. She tore down the old brick house, which was unpretentious and substantial; and, with the aid of the architect, Roy Miller, she built what appears to be a replica of Mount Vernon but is really a copy of Catherine's ancestral home in Virginia. In Tennessee, strife has developed between Tom and his mother; and they have divided their farm by putting a fence through the middle of it. Tom runs his half, and Mrs. Manigault runs hers; and no question exists about which is the better manager. Elsie Manigault, who raises horses, makes one mistake after another; and her only salvation from disaster is an almost endless supply of money.

Elsie Manigault is one of those rigid, aggressive, vain, cold, and beautiful women who are encountered in other of Miss Gordon's books. Having abdicated the usual duties and responsibilities of womanhood—the caring for a household, the rearing of children—she has no real life or culture of her own, or nothing to which she is deeply committed. All she has is money and the desire to run things. Her son, Tom, being a real man, resists his mother's attempts to dominate him and that naturally displeases her. Behind this attempt at domination, Miss Gordon shows, is an attempt to emasculate her son. What Elsie Manigault really prefers are effeminate men, like the architect Roy Miller, who kisses her hand and praises her figure—without involving her in any meaningful emotional relationship.

Tom, ideally, is the kind of man Catherine ought, under other circumstances, to have married. He is physically powerful, capable of action and of taking Catherine, even of driving Roy Miller off the place when he discovers him involved in a homosexual relationship with a houseboy. But Tom is not Catherine's "fate." He is younger than she; and, more important, he has been damaged by his mother. Catherine sees that, despite his masculine assertiveness, Tom is still emotionally tied to his mother: "The enchantment fell too early and her features are the most glamorous that he will ever see and will always be harking back to that brightest moment of danger."[12] This perception loosens Tom's hold over Catherine and causes her to think, "I have made a mistake...I have taken the wrong road and it is too late to turn back."[13] It is not too late, however. The return of Willy and the death of the stallion alter the atmosphere at Swan Quarter. When Catherine is left with only her husband to turn to, the road back to life is clearly marked out for her.

III *Universal Implications*

Jim Chapman, who symbolizes Catherine's true fate, is Miss Gordon's chief means of extending the implications of her story into the world outside the novel. He is also the most complex and interesting of these characters. Chapman is a Midwesterner from Mount Hope, Ohio, but his father was a transplanted Vermonter, a doctor who had never felt at home in Ohio. "The Ohio farmer who had accumulated enough money sold his farm and came to town to live out the rest of his days," Doctor Chapman observed; but a Vermont farmer "would stay by his land till he died and then have to be carried off feet first."[14] Jim Chapman speculates, "was there something in the [Ohio] land itself that repelled human attachment? Perhaps it was too fertile. Roots put down easily are not as enduring as those which make their way through the interstices of rock.... Middle Westerners springing out of the rich black loam of the prairie, are always on their way somewhere else..."[15] Whether the author agrees with Jim's musings about the quality of Midwestern soil (and Jim's perceptions are not always to be trusted) is beside the point, for Jim and his problem become, by the end of the novel, the embodiment of a more widespread human one.

Jim Chapman is a historian, an intellectual, a man with no meaningful past of his own. He is drawn to older cultures and to people from them because he senses qualities in them that he himself does not possess. They are people with a strong sense of their own identity, a knowledge of the past—particularly of their own ancestors—a feeling of kinship with their families, and a love of their own particular spot of earth. Chapman himself realizes his deficiencies: "The truth is that I have no character ... I have no prejudice . . . no instincts, no convictions that are readily translatable into action."[16] And, when he encounters the face of someone who has the qualities that he lacks, a face "alert, disciplined, histrionic rather than contemplative," he wants to "shatter" it.[17]

Though a historian, Jim Chapman is also something of a poet. At least, he has a poet's feeling for language, and he gives expression to what are by now rather commonplace views of the general human condition. For example, as he is walking about New York, Chapman pauses and looks up at the "great building whose lighted windows jewelled the dark": "All over the city, people in their cubicles of stone or concrete or steel, lay as tight against one another as bees in their cells of wax, and even beyond the confines of the island the great, crowded ramparts flung themselves on and on until if one travelled far enough one might come to a building whose four walls housed one man and his wife and children."[18] He implicitly compares the lives of people living in cramped apartments to "Bees, in their solitary cells, [who] do not control their own destinies" and then he is moved to a rhapsody of despair and decay:

And the queen? O City, preparing for what strange nuptial flight! Having stung her sisters to death, she rises on rapid wing, but when the dead bridegroom has dropped from between her feathery legs she will hurtle down, past the heaped bodies of dead and dying drones. Will not the odor of decay penetrate the royal chamber, interrupting even the processes of fecundation, so that, seeking a cleaner air, she may lead her hive forth in a last flight, in which, traveling high above the orchards and the gardens, they will not stop to cull honey from the apple blossom or the rose, but will continue on, an insensate mass, until, dying, falling in a great cloud, they darken with their wings the whole west?[19]

Jim Chapman is a poet of the *Waste Land* school, and Miss Gordon shows that his vision is to some extent an accurate reflection of a moral confusion implicit in the lives of some of these characters, particularly in Jim himself. Indeed, Jim must be seen, in part at least, as responsible for the waste land in which he lives. He is incapable of acting; he can only feel and analyze his predicament; he cannot struggle against it. There are times, we are told, "when in an illusion that was part dream, part waking he seemed to be suspended precariously over an immense pit. He half knew what lurked in its depths, but his concern was not with avoiding the descent; he rallied his febrile energies in order that he might experience the fall. His detachment from the scene was the ultimate horror."[20]

This realization takes place on the train while he is traveling from New York to Swan Quarter to see Catherine. During the trip, Chapman encounters two young men, both Southerners, men of action. One young man is apparently the editor of a large-circulation magazine; the other is an air force officer; both of them, with their vitality, their self-assurance, and their ability to act, make Chapman acutely aware of his own deficiencies. It is the soldier in particular that he envies. "I wish I was one of them," he thinks, "for it is something, in this life, for a man to know where he is going, even if the appointment is with the minotaur."[21]

The scene that most forcefully drives home to the reader, if not to Chapman, the terrible nature of his failure occurs in the wood near Swan Quarter. He and Catherine have confronted each other; and Catherine, rather defiantly, has blurted out the fact of her infidelity. In his fury, produced not by outraged principles or by jealousy but by the inhuman, almost mechanical desire to see suffering in Catherine's eyes, Jim chokes her. She fights her way free. Jim, somewhat stunned and shaken, leaves the house and enters the woods. There he flings himself down beside a spring. As he lies there, he relives the recent past and longingly contemplates a suicide that he is too cowardly to commit. He stands then as though "to go back." "Back to what?" he says; and, as he does so, a shadow detaches itself from the foliage and moves into the light. In a moment, Chapman sees a man's figure with a pack on his back, and he then recognizes him as a pioneer forebear of

Catherine's who had settled this part of the country. He is the son of Irish John Lewis to whom the land on which he stands was deeded after the Revolutionary War.[22]

This remarkably effective scene—particularly since it ought not to work at all—deserves a detailed examination. The best way to appreciate what Miss Gordon does is to consider the scene in the light of what is needed at this point in the novel. This episode is to be the turning point in Jim's life or, to use Miss Gordon's term, the peripety (actually, the change in Jim's fortune began earlier on the train); and, after this scene, Chapman is to be aware of the extent of his failure and is to return to his wife. What is needed is a dramatic confrontation that will precipitate the change but one which will grow out of and be consistent with the setting, with the scenes that have preceded it, and with Jim's character. Miss Gordon's choice is seriously limited by her setting, for what could happen at Swan Quarter that could lift the veil from Chapman's eyes? There is the emotional bout with Catherine and his flight to the woods, but what could possibly happen there that would bring him to the brink of self-knowledge?

The obvious solution would be an interior monologue in which Jim is made to sort through past experience and find the proper answer, but that is not Miss Gordon's method. She wants the recognition to grow out of a real encounter; the struggle must be externalized. And her solution is as ingenious as it is effective: she has Jim encounter a figure from the past, an ancestor of his wife's; and, though this figure may be conjured up by Jim's disordered brain (Miss Gordon does not clear up the mystery; indeed she is not concerned about that), it has nevertheless, in the fictional sense, a literal reality. John Lewis' son is brought before our eyes, a silent man in buckskin who builds a fire and cooks the bloody tongue of a buffalo. Then, after he has been seen, Miss Gordon has him rest beside his fire while Chapman harangues him: "The land is cursed, it is an old land, ruled by a goddess whose limbs were weary with turning before Ireland rose from the sea. An ancient goddess whom men have awakened from an evil dream. . . ."[23]

As Chapman speaks, the shadowy figure regards him with a mocking eye:

"It is No Man's Land . . . That is the enchantment. The land will turn brittle and fall away from under your children's feet, they will have no fixed habitation, will hold no one spot dearer than another, will roam as savage as the buffalo that now flees your arquebus. And the demons!... They will be guarded and served by demons. But the demons will not have the grace, as in ages past, to assume half-human forms, but will retain their own inhuman shapes? Sticks, stones, pulleys, levers such as Archimedes devised, will have voices, show frowning visages. And your children, languid, pale, their numbers withered, will bow down before them and when they speak their voices will not be heard for the inhuman babble of their gods."[24]

This meaning of this scene is suggested by the gestures of the man from the pioneer past. He lays down the morsel of flesh that he has been eating, takes up his pack and rifle, and moves toward the stream. For his kind—the man of action, principle, and courage, whether of the present or the past—the type of warning uttered by Chapman is without meaning. For Chapman's "Waste Land" vision is simply the mirror image of his own inner life. He mistakes his personal dilemma for a general human one.

Chapman recovers from his paralysis, however. After his encounter in the woods with the spirit of John Lewis, he stumbles back to the house; and, after a series of small gestures, he and Catherine are reconciled. Then he kneels and kisses the instep of Catherine's foot. This gesture is that of a repentant husband, but it is also Miss Gordon's way of dramatizing the fact that Jim Chapman has reached "out to a world outside himself—that world which, from time immemorial has been personified in the feminine consciousness."[25] In resuming his responsibilities as his wife's husband, he has acted in a meaningful and, for him, a heroic way.

Though Jim Chapman is the technical hero of the novel, Catherine is closer to the paradigm. She is the spiritual as well as the lineal heir of John Lewis. She has the principles in this family, and she is the one who first acts on principle. She leaves her husband when she discovers that he has been unfaithful to her. She does enter into a love affair with another man; but, when she realizes what life with that man would be like, she turns him away. And, at the end of the novel, she makes it possible for her husband to return to her. She greets him on the steps of the house at Swan Quarter and prepares for him a symbolic cup. The cup contains coffee rather than wine, but it serves the purpose. She is ready to resume her domestic duties. If it is a man's duty to act and to lead, it is a wife's to respond and follow. It is this principle that lies behind Catherine's conduct toward the close of the novel.

Had she chosen Tom Manigault rather than her husband, she would have abandoned the high road for the moral wilderness; and, though this wilderness might have been delightful for a time, Catherine would eventually have lost her way without a compass to guide her and would have become another of the strange women on the porch.

The Women on the Porch is an impressive performance and deserves to be better known to students of American fiction. In the history of Caroline Gordon's development as a novelist, it is of great importance; for it marks a new departure in her fiction. In her earlier work, as we have seen, the search for a hero confined her largely to the past; and in *The Garden of Adonis*, her one novel set completely in the contemporary world, she depends heavily upon her hero's connections to the premodern world. Thus, it could be said that Miss Gordon has always avoided a confrontation with the modern myth—until *Women on the Porch*. In this novel, she meets the myth head-on. True, in her use of John Lewis, she depends again on history; but the main issue of the novel is worked out in the actions of Jim Chapman as he moves from a paralyzed hero to a man of action. Miss Gordon's strategy is to grant the reality of the "Waste Land" world but to show that it is primarily a reflection of an inner rather than an outer world.

There are, of course, arguments that can be brought against this position—such as the irreducible reality of the "Waste Land" to the men who see the world in this way; but that is an abyss into which Miss Gordon refuses to look very intently. For, as she might argue, once the reality of this subjective vision is admitted, the paralysis must also be accepted. Miss Gordon's strategy, furthermore, is to give several perspectives on the "Waste Land" world. We see that world through the eyes of Chapman but we also see Jim Chapman from outside, and as a result see how much of that world is the product of his background and his sensibility. Also, we see another world, that of Swan Quarter, which might have been presented as a "Waste Land" but is not. Indeed, Miss Gordon suggests through symbolic imagery that the three women on the porch and the subterranean world that they inhabit is as old as Western civilization itself. We are not to think of Swan Quarter as the "decadent South" nor even as decadent twentieth-century civilization. It is, rather, another instance of the kind of underworld that has existed in all times and all places where there has been a like failure of will.

V. *Conclusion*

The experience of Catherine at Swan Quarter, her early involvement with the life there, her affair with Tom Manigault, the Manigault establishment with a woman in possession of the land and men relegated to positions of inferiority and subservience to women—all of these perversions of the natural order act as a backdrop for Catherine's final act: the rejection of this world. Catherine's actions and the final perspective we get of the life-in-death world of Swan Quarter cast a strong light on the "Waste Land" world of Jim Chapman. Moreover, Chapman's experience is not unique in literary history. There have been other men in other times and other places faced with similar problems. The crucial difference has been in the way men have responded.

Early in the novel Jim Chapman thinks of a student he had once helped translate Dante, and he quotes to himself the lines at the beginning of the "Inferno:"

In the middle of the journey of our life I came to myself in a dark wood where the straight way was lost.

. . .

I cannot rightly tell how I entered it, so full of sleep was I about the moment that I lost the true way . . .[26]

These lines (a foreshadowing of the later scene in which Jim Chapman encounters John Lewis) do more than tell us that Jim Chapman is living in a kind of hell, though that is certainly part of their function. They tell us, too, the reason for Jim's having lost his way: he has nothing to guide him through the dark woods, nothing but his own unaided intellect. This reference to Dante also indicates that the kind of problem confronting Jim Chapman was also faced by another intellectual in another age. Dante, to be sure, found the "true way," and Jim does not. He does at least find his way out of the woods of Swan Quarter and reestablishes his marriage with Catherine, but in a sense he is still wondering about the mouth of hell.

The problems raised in *Women on the Porch* and the solution alluded to by the reference to the *Divine Comedy* are a foreshadowing of the direction that Miss Gordon's fiction and her own life were in the near future to take.

CHAPTER 9

A Christian Fairy Tale

BETWEEN the publication of *The Women on the Porch* and the writing of *The Strange Children* (1951), Caroline Gordon became a Roman Catholic. In her fiction, we find little to prepare us for this decision; for there is no explicit concern with religious issues in her first eight novels, and the heroes of those books are not what we regard as typically Christian types. But Caroline Gordon is not typical of her times. Novelists who create what— in the jargon of a certain kind of modern criticism—are called "Christ figures" are attracted to the romantic possibilities of the prime Christian personality. They do not see linked with this personality (Jesus) the workaday and often too familiar moral and ascetic aspects of Christianity—perhaps because these aspects are, after all, the ones more important to Christians. For if these qualities are acknowledged at all in modern fiction, it is usually to disparage them. It is traditional Christianity, however, that Miss Gordon has been attracted by: to the Church as an institution; to the moral code of the Christian commitment; to the asceticism, the mysticism, and the redemptive promise of Christian faith. All of these matters, it is possible to judge, are better served within the Catholic faith than outside it. When that circumstance is understood, Miss Gordon's conversion to Catholicism seems not only quite logical but even inevitable.

From the beginning of her career, Caroline Gordon has been implicitly a religious writer. Her novels and short stories, in effect, raise the question: how can I be saved from the abyss that yawns at the feet of every mortal?[1] This question was asked in the first story Miss Gordon published, "Summer Dust."[2] The small girl of that story finds her answer in the words of a fairy godmother who holds out the hope of a crown and of a gorgeous robe for those who reject self-indulgence. Hers is, of course, a non-Christian answer to the question; but, if we press the answer of the "god-mother" a little further, religious implications arise. Is any "hell" at our feet to be understood in secular terms only? For that matter, is any body of morality to be understood so? These questions, properly understood, point toward an acceptance of the entire body of Christian faith. We can suggest that, as an artist, Miss Gordon has stopped picking and choosing.

In most of Caroline Gordon's subsequent stories and novels that same question is raised, usually in secular terms; but the answers are never without religious implications. It is not simply martial prowess that Miss Gordon admires in General Nathan Bedford Forrest or in his fictional counterpart Rives Allard; neither is it merely the aristocratic quality of John Llewellyn, Fontaine Allard, or Ben Allard that is depicted for our admiration. It is, rather, the capacity of these heroes for self-sacrifice, for giving themselves to an ideal. Thus the brave deed—whether it be a child's turning her back on evil and walking through the dark woods alone, a Negro farmhand's outfacing a white man's attempt to besmirch his honor, a soldier's snatching a regimental flag from a retreating color bearer, or a proud man's kissing the instep of his wife's foot—is, somehow, a redemptive act.[3] In *The Strange Children* and *The Malefactors*, Miss Gordon moves to "redemptive acts" firmly placed in a perspective where we can speak really rather than metaphorically of redemption.

As to how these acts are redemptive Miss Gordon does not explicitly say, but the whole bent of her talent has been to get us to see and to make us feel that they are. The lucid style, the illusion of an objectively created world, and the appeal to history, to cultural anthropology, to Classical myth have been resorted to with the aim of convincing us in ways that the author has at various times believed ought to convince. And yet, as Miss Gordon's religious conversion seems to imply, the realism and the historical and Classical paradigms have not been wholly satisfactory—not because they are false but primarily because they do not rest on authority that is valid for the present as well as for the past. She wants to move from anticipations of the effect of redemption to redemption itself: an experience that implies a religious context instead of a mythological or "secular culture" approximation of that context. The problem is illustrated in *Women on the Porch*, which was written just before Miss Gordon's religious conversion. In it, part of her strategy is to have Jim Chapman move from a state of paralysis and estrangement from his wife to action and reconciliation. What precipitates the reconciliation is Chapman's dramatic confrontation with his wife's pioneer forebear. The act of reconciliation, the kissing of the wife's instep, though clear enough on the level of intention, is, ultimately, meaningless. It signifies nothing more than a momentary self-abasement. What the gesture needed, if I may so state, is a tradition behind it. When, for example, Rives Allard snatches up a flag in *None Shall Come Back*, the weight of the whole Southern cause rides on the gesture. Rives's gesture "works" because we understand not only what led up to it but also the outcome since that is a matter of history. True, that kind of historical act can work as a reminder for those in the modern world, but it cannot be a blueprint for renewed action in the present. *The Strange Children* and *The Malefactors* represent Miss Gordon's study of a blueprint that she regards as authentic and full.

I   *The Main Plot*

The narrator of *The Strange Children* is Lucy Lewis, granddaughter of Aleck Maury and the daughter of Stephen and Sarah Lewis who appeared years earlier in *Aleck Maury, Sportsman* and later in "Old Red." Like her grandfather, Lucy has a sharp eye for the follies of other people, and she is very aware of how inconsistent adults are. She notices that her mother opens her mouth too wide when she talks, and she is quick to point out to her mother when *she* tells a lie. Lucy also has a dignity, an innocence, and a natural intelligence that set her apart from everyone else in the book, particularly from the self-conscious and somewhat pretentious adults. She likes things and people because of what they are in themselves, not because they are like or unlike something else. For example, she feels drawn to a family of poor whites who are tenants on her family's farm, and she is quick to sense that they are being patronized by a visiting Northerner. She is able to see the tenants as they are in their ramshackle house and in their somewhat "trashy" condition (which the Northern visitor would like to see alleviated); but she can still admire and even envy them for having what she cannot have: a sense of family unity and cohesion.

Despite her very attractive qualities, her almost intuitive moral sense, and the fact that the point of view is closely identified with her throughout most of the novel, Lucy is not the moral gauge by which the other characters are to be judged. For in Miss Gordon's vision, Lucy's point of view is necessarily limited: first, because she is a child; second, because she lacks what the children of the poor white family have to guide them, a religious faith. Part of the author's strategy, as we shall see, is to get the reader to identify with Lucy's point of view in order to expose the limitations of mere unaided natural goodness.

Strange Children begins with Lucy sitting in the window seat in the dining room of the house at Benfolly, a farm near Gloversville, Tennessee. Stephen Lewis is in his study working on his book about the Civil War. Sarah Lewis, his wife and Lucy's mother, has just received a telephone call from an old friend who has announced that he is driving out to see them. When the old friend, Tubby McColum, arrives in a green convertible, Lucy is smitten by his charm and gallantry. He calls her "Sabrina fair," lifts her up into the air, and, somewhat later, takes her for a walk in the woods and carves their names on a tree. But "Uncle" Tubby's attentions are quickly diverted by the arrival of two more friends, Kevin Reardon and his wife Isabel whom the Lewises have not seen for a number of years. It becomes evident even before the Reardon's arrival that there is something unusual, even mysterious about this couple. After their arrival, it also becomes clear that there is something going on between Tubby and Isabel.

Kevin Reardon, we learn, is a very rich man who has lived for years in France. His father made an immense fortune on the stock market, then gave up business and subsequently became religious. Reardon's parents were divorced and for many years he did not see his father who lived on a secluded estate in southern France. Then, on an impulse, Reardon went to visit his father. He was so repelled by the old man's religious piety that he walked out without spending the night and without even saying good-bye. After his father's death, however, Reardon too became religious and he has now returned to America to assist in setting up a contemplative order.

Reardon's wife Isabel was a promising poet when she married Reardon, but she has now ceased to write. She is the daughter of a Minnesota farmer and grew up seven miles outside of Saint Paul. Tubby McCollum, who has recently visited the Reardon's at Saint Tropez in France and stayed with them several months, tells the Lewises that Isabel and Reardon are not getting along well together. Isabel is disturbed by his preoccupation with religion, and particularly with his plan to give his money to a religious order. As Tubby tells the story, it appears that Reardon is unkind, even cruel, to Isabel and that he keeps her locked up at home so that her friends could not visit her. Steve and Sarah Lewis, to

whom Tubby tells most of this story, become aware that Tubby
and Isabel have been having an affair and that they have arranged to meet at the Lewises' in order to continue it. The
Lewises, of course, are prevented by their position as hosts from
interfering. All they can do is to stand by and speculate about
what is happening. What eventually happens is that Tubby and
Isabel elope.

II   *Lucy's Story*

The story of the Reardons and Tubby McColum occurs in the
background. In the foreground is Lucy who hears—often overhears—and sees what is transpiring in the adult world; but Lucy
also has her own adventures. Shortly after the arrival of the
Reardons, Lucy wanders into the bedroom occupied by Reardon,
impulsively picks up a beautiful and valuable crucifix, and carries it off to her own room. Later, when she sees Reardon, Lucy
is uneasy and self-conscious; during dinner, when he is pleasant
to her, she resolves to return the crucifix to him. When circumstances prevent her from putting it back in his room, she forgets
for a time that she still has it. Later, when Reardon asks if she
has seen it, Lucy suggests that the Negro maid Jenny might have
taken it. It is not until Lucy discovers that Reardon has offered
to buy her a pony that she becomes acutely uncomfortable about
the stolen crucifix. After Reardon's wife leaves him, Lucy returns
the crucifix and confesses that it was she, not Jenny, who had
taken it.

The protagonist of the novel is, of course, Lucy; and, technically
speaking, the background of the visitors and the conflicts among
the adults are part of the complication of the action in which Lucy
is involved. I do not imply, however, that the issues of the adult
world are not of major importance; they are. But these conflicts
are brought into focus principally through Lucy's experiences.
Indeed, when reading this novel on the allegorical level, we might
classify Lucy as a kind of innocent young Everyman setting out
on the road of life. On the way, she encounters forces of good and
evil contending for possession of her soul: the evil ones, those
represented by Isabel and Tubby; the good by Kevin Reardon.
The decision that Lucy makes, to follow Reardon rather than
Tubby, provides both a resolution of the action and, implicitly, a
comment on the issues raised by the conduct of the adults.

One of the main technical problems that confronted Miss Gordon in writing *Strange Children* was how to emphasize or clarify the deeper issues of the action without violating Lucy's point of view. At the close of the novel, Miss Gordon switches from Lucy's point of view to Stephen Lewis'; but, up until that point, she confines herself wholly to Lucy's point of view. Her ways of getting around Lucy's limited perception are various, but the most elaborate is through the use of a fairy tale that to some extent parallels the characters and the events in *The Strange Children*. The first reference to the fairy tale occurs in Chapter 1. Lucy is reading *Undine,* and before the close of the chapter, we are aware that the strangers who visit the Lewis farm are strange people indeed. Readers familiar with *Undine* are also made aware before the novel closes that the events of that story and those of *Strange Children* are significantly related.

Undine, it is useful to note, is a fairy tale about a fisherman and his wife who, after they lose their child by drowning, are visited by Undine, a capricious, roguish maiden, who comes mysteriously to them and is reared by them in the place of their lost child. A knight, Huldbrand von Ringstetten, takes shelter in their cottage and falls in love with Undine. They are married, and Undine in consequence receives a soul. But her relatives, particularly her Uncle Kuhleborn, a wicked water goblin, cause trouble. Huldbrand neglects Undine and becomes interested in the proud Bertolda, who is humbled when she discovers that she is the lost child of the fisherman and his wife. One day in a boat on the Danube, Huldbrand, tormented by Undine's kindred, rebukes his wife; and she is snatched away from him into the water and is seen no more. Huldbrand proposes to Bertolda, and they are about to be married when Undine rises from a well, goes to the knight's room, and kisses him; and, as a consequence, he dies.

The parallels between the two works are not exact, and the endings are different, but a number of important similarities exist. The arrival of Uncle Tubby at Benfolly, which comes at the beginning of the book, is rather like the arrival of Huldbrand von Ringstetten at the home of Undine's foster parents; however Tubby's character is much more like that of Undine's Uncle Kuhleborn, the wicked water goblin. The connection of Tubby to Kuhleborn is suggested by words italicized in the following quotation: "A big, curly-headed man sat at the wheel. His coffee-colored suit was splashed here and there, as if he had driven *through the river* instead of over it."[4] The parallel is continued as the action begins to unfold. Uncle Tubby seems to have an extraordinary fondness for water. He visits the waterfall in the woods near Benfolly, takes Isabel and Lucy swimming, and is fascinated by the river that flows underground in the caves beneath the Lewis farm.

The parallel of Isabel Reardon to Undine is even clearer, for it is significant that Isabel's first poem was titled "Water Bearer" and that, though she is not drawn to the water as Tubby is (she shivers when the underground river is mentioned), she permits Tubby to take her swimming. Like Undine, Isabel is "tortured" by her husband; she weeps and, again like Undine, is carried off from her husband—by Uncle Tubby. And, though Isabel is not a changeling as Undine was, she was clearly an unusual child for a Minnesota farmer to have borne. She is as roguish and as capricious as Undine and is never completely tamed.[5] Kevin Reardon, who most resembles the knight Huldbrand, is a Christian gentleman of high estate, or what passes for it in the modern world; and he falls in love and marries the beautiful, unusual daughter of humble people. His wife, whom he has rescued from her soulless existence, is snatched from him by her spiritual "kin." Reardon's attachment, however, is to the Virgin rather than to a mortal woman. He does not die at the end of the novel, as Huldbrand does, but is simply stunned and grieved by the loss of his wife.

The parallels between *Undine* and *Strange Children* are not thoroughly developed in the novel, nor are they meant to be; for Miss Gordon is not depending upon the earlier work to give her novel external structure. What parallels there are direct us toward other levels of meaning, particularly the moral; for the parallels are the author's way of making a moral judgment on actions that would seem to lie beyond the reach of such judgment. Since Tubby and Isabel are not Christians, Sarah Lewis says of Isabel, "the ordinary canons don't apply" to them; but Miss Gordon, by linking them imaginatively to the underworld of water spirits and by setting them in opposition to Christian values, has suggested a moral judgment. What Isabel and Tubby have done is evil not just because it has violated the Sixth Commandment, or the sacredness of the marriage vows, but because their affair is selfish and destructive of other human beings.

Like the author of *Undine*, Miss Gordon establishes conflicts between people from an underworld and characters who represent Christian virtues, and Kevin Reardon, of course, represents the latter. Before his conversion, Reardon had a vision in which the Virgin Mary appeared to him as he lies with a broken leg beside his wrecked automobile. His sense of her immense and monu-

mental presence lends him the physical and moral strength neces-
ary to drag himself to a nearby spring and eventually to save
himself and his wife. That same presence, which he later tries to
ignore, remains beside him. There are obvious strategic difficulties
in presenting such a religious experience in a novel that is so
firmly anchored in the real world, particularly for readers who are
also likely to be as skeptical of religious visions as they are of fairy
tales.

However, Miss Gordon employs strategies calculated to circum-
vent these difficulties. Instead of presenting Reardon's religious
experience directly, she doubly removes it from the reader's view
by having Sarah Lewis, who has heard the story from Reardon,
relate it to her husband. Then, in order to accommodate the kind
of objections that readers might make, Miss Gordon has Steve
Lewis remain skeptical. Sarah is convinced, but Steve neither believes nor disbelieves; he merely cites historical accounts of visions
and instantaneous conversions. Sarah, angered by her husband's
skepticism and by his purely intellectual response, quarrels with
him: "You know everything, don't you? . . . Just mention anything
and you can tell us about something else somewhere just exactly
like it . . ."[6] Sarah's anger is convincing. She and her husband have
quarreled before, and the conflict between them is part of the
unhappy reality of their daughter Lucy's world. But Sarah's anger
is also a rather clever device to disguise the fact that Lewis'
intellectual response is being disparaged.

Sarah's attack is also a defense of Kevin Reardon's visions: if
there have been historical accounts of visions and instantaneous
conversions, then why not one in our own day? Unsympathetic
readers, of course, will not be convinced by that kind of argument;
and Kevin Reardon's vision will be dismissed as, at best, halluci-
nation; at worst, as a kind of insanity. But with this attitude Miss
Gordon also comes to grips. Indeed, it might be said that she
structures the novel to raise the question as to which characters
are sane and then provides the answer.

It is through the relationship of Kevin-Isabel-Tubby that the question is raised, but it is through Lucy's relationship with these other
characters that the answer is provided. The question about Isabel's
sanity is first raised when Tubby tells the Lewises that Reardon
keeps Isabel locked up and will not let her friends visit her. Tubby
suggests that Reardon is mistreating his wife. The first real indi-
cation that Isabel is indeed mad comes to the reader during a
game of charades played in the Lewises' living room. Isabel par-

ticipates in a tableau contrived by Tubby that Reardon regards as blasphemous. During the performance, Isabel goes berserk; and, when Reardon subdues her, Tubby regards Reardon's actions as cruel and inhuman and attempts to interfere. Indeed, the suspicion that it is Reardon rather than Isabel who is insane is introduced through Lucy. She not only thinks that Kevin Reardon is the strangest man she has ever known but decides that *"He's crazy. That's what they've been talking about all along. He's crazy."*[7] By using Lucy in this way, Miss Gordon is exploiting Lucy's limited powers of perception and is also preparing for the final revelations that Isabel is indeed crazy and that Tubby is both depraved and insane for eloping with a madwoman. "'Did you ever tell [Tubby] she was mad?'" Sarah Lewis asks. Reardon replies, "'I tried to, once. . . .'"[8] But Tubby had not believed him.

The deep immorality of what Tubby has done is developed through Lucy's relationship with Kevin Reardon on the one hand and with Isabel and Tubby on the other. These two sets of characters may be considered as forces from another world contending for the soul of an individual mortal, for that of Lucy, the prize. Clearly, she is attracted to Uncle Tubby. It might even be said, though Miss Gordon does not say it, that Lucy "falls in love" with Tubby. When Tubby begins paying attention to Isabel, Lucy is hurt and humiliated; but she likes Isabel, too. Moreover, there is a resemblance in appearance and in actions between Lucy and Isabel. Isabel is aware of this resemblance; and, as part of her campaign to win Lucy, she heightens it. They both have long, blonde hair and are slender and small; Isabel dresses herself in the same colors that Lucy wears. Isabel and Lucy are both somewhat capricious and willful; and, as children are likely to be, they are concerned only with the gratification of their own desires. Isabel is, of course, not a child; but she has never grown up. She has never been made to suffer disappointment and, consequently, has never developed the ability to love selflessly. This quality she shares with Undine, her fairy-tale counterpart.

The fact that Lucy acts like a child is not alarming, of course, since that's what she is. But the question raised by the struggle over Lucy is whether she will mature or will remain, like Isabel, a spoiled child. Her parents make few demands upon her, and Lucy is for a time openly attracted to the secret, self-indulgent underworld of Tubby and Isabel and is repelled by Reardon and the demands of his world. Unlike Uncle Tubby, who pays her flattering compliments, Reardon is quiet and preoccupied. He drives over to Gloversville every afternoon at three o'clock to say the Stations of the Cross. And, as we have seen, Lucy even concludes that he is crazy; but, at the same time that Lucy is afraid and suspicious of Reardon, she is also subconsciously attracted to him and symbolically to what he represents. This attitude is dramatized in her theft of Reardon's crucifix.

During dinner the evening of the guests' arrival at Benfolly, the discussion centers on religious subjects; and the question of "Holy Roller" theology comes up. Lucy, who is friendly with a poor-white family, the MacDonoughs, who are Holy Rollers, is asked to explain their religion. Uncle Tubby puts his arm about Lucy's shoulder and, drawing her close to him and shaking her a little, says, "Come on, *belle dame,* speak a few words [in the Unknown Tongue]!"[9] Lucy disengages herself from Tubby's embrace and, while explaining what she knows, steals a glance at Reardon. She feels as she looks at him, smiling with his head on one side, that he is considering how best to do her a kindness. Then she thinks that, of course, he does not know the crucifix is missing because he has not been back to his room. When Lucy immediately decides that she will take the crucifix from its hiding place and return it, that thought makes her so happy she feels like singing.

Lucy is delayed by her mother, who insists that she help clear the table; and then, as she runs upstairs to replace the crucifix, she is stopped by Isabel who draws her into her bedroom and presents her with a gift, a little cloisonné box which is just the right size to hold the crucifix. Lucy thinks "Do you suppose *she's giving it to me because she knows I've got the little man?*"[10] When Lucy goes back downstairs with Isabel, she learns that the adults are going to play charades and that she will be permitted to stay up and watch. She thinks that, in the confusion of the game, she will be able to slip into Reardon's room and drop the crucifix on the floor beside his bed. But, in the excitement that follows, Lucy forgets about returning it; and, by the time the evening is over, she has decided that Reardon is crazy and is no longer concerned about not having returned the crucifix.

That night as Lucy sleeps she has a dream that dramatizes her predicament. She and her father and mother are walking through a forest "such as the Knight Huldbrand had wandered in, but the road was not plain and every now and then they stopped, not knowing which way to turn." Her father, who is walking with his head up, will not listen to her mother who says that the trail goes "this way." The mother leaves her father and goes away. When she comes back, her hands are full of white flowers. Lucy's father does not respond to his wife; instead, he points to another way down, one on which Mrs. Reardon and Mr. Reardon and Uncle Tubby are coming. Mrs. Reardon is in white and is carrying a tray on which reposes a head that is muttering; and, when Uncle Tubby and Mr. Reardon hear what the lips are saying, they cry out and run away. But Mrs. Reardon keeps walking forward. The trees get thinner and thinner, and Lucy sees that the country she and her parents are walking through is not really country at all; it is only the brink of a great chasm into which they will fall if they do not turn back.[11]

Lucy's dream also dramatizes the central conflict of the novel. The way taken by Mrs. Reardon in the dream represents the evil way of life being taken by a number of characters in the novel; and the path taken by Sarah, who returns with her hands full of white flowers, is the other way, the one represented by Kevin Reardon, the spiritual way. Lucy too is looking down the wrong path. It is not just her theft of the crucifix or the fact that she is attracted to Tubby; the point is that she is beginning to see life as Isabel and Tubby see it. This fact is suggested by her belief that Reardon is crazy, and by her accompanying Tubby and Isabel on a swimming party and her leaving them only because her mother calls her home.

III   The Two Plots Related

Lucy eventually finds the right path as a result of being administered two rather severe shocks. The first occurs when she and her friend Lois and the cook Jenny wander into a thicket looking for blackberries and come upon Tubby and Isabel in a sexual embrace. Lucy does not fully understand what is happening; but, as she looks into Tubby's eyes, she sees in them a profound self-deception: "his gaze had merely happened to fall upon her face. He had seen her and he had not seen her. And if she and the others had not stood there he would have stared straight before him in the same way, as if he were looking beyond whatever was before him, at something that was not there and never could be there, no matter if you looked all your life."[12] After this encounter, Lucy confronts her parents who are arguing about the nature of Reardon's vision. As we have seen, her mother believes in it enthusiastically; her father, in his skepticism, reaches for historical parallels. When Lucy rushes from the room where her parents are arguing and leaves them there together, she almost immediately encounters the person from whom she is attempting to flee, Kevin Reardon, who asks whether she has seen the lost crucifix. As we have observed, Lucy gives Reardon the impression that Jenny, the Negro maid, is the culprit.

The next shock administered to Lucy is of a different order. It is the gift of a pony that she had been wanting all summer, but it comes from the man she has wronged. On the way to the country, Lucy's mother tells her that Mr. Reardon has asked to pay for the pony. Lucy is staggered; this gift clearly marks the trail before her: "She would not turn her head. There was no use looking back now." Lucy wonders whether Mr. Reardon knew about the crucifix "back there" when she lied and told him Jenny had probably taken it. She concludes that "he knew something that she didn't know. Was this it?"[13]

As it turns out, Reardon had not known that Lucy took the crucifix. When Lucy herself tells him, Reardon is astonished to hear that she is the thief. When he speaks to her about it, his voice is harsh; but, when he sees her tears, he softens and puts his arm about her shoulders. When Lucy's mother asks what ails Lucy, Reardon replies, "Nothing. She's all right." Lucy it seems, is more than all right; for she is well on her way to discovering what Mr. Reardon knows that she does not know. The stealing and the return of the crucifix symbolize this discovery. When Lucy takes the crucifix she is smitten by its physical beauty; but, on a deeper psychological level she, as we have noted, is unconsciously attracted to the way of life symbolized by the crucifix. This attraction is suggested by her response to Reardon at dinner the evening of the Reardon's arrival at Benfolly. But Lucy is also attracted to the wild, self-indulgent life represented by Isabel and symbolized by the cloisonné box that Isabel has given Lucy; and it is during this period that Isabel's hold on Lucy is strongest and that Lucy thinks Reardon crazy.

In a subtle way, the crucifix Lucy has stolen draws her into a relationship with Reardon somewhat analogous to the relationship of Isabel and Reardon. In stealing from her parent's guest, Lucy has violated a sacred trust. Moreover, in keeping the crucifix and allowing the blame to fall on Jenny, Lucy has committed an injustice to another human being and has betrayed the man who has befriended her. In returning the crucifix, Lucy not only atones for her sin; she also manifests other important Christian virtues. In the first place, her action is prompted by compassion, for she gives the crucifix back not because she is afraid she will be found out, nor through pride masking as humility, but because Reardon is visibly suffering because of the loss of his wife. Moreover, Lucy might have lied and allowed Jenny to take the blame; instead, she confesses her guilt and takes as her punishment Reardon's reproach. It might be said that Lucy has made her confession and that Reardon has been both the injured party and also her confessor.

In analyzing this scene, I have made the symbolism of the crucifix seem rather mechanical, which it is not. Miss Gordon establishes the action so firmly on the literal level that the reader is not immediately aware of the meaning as I have explained it. The return of the crucifix assumes meaning only after the reader is made to feel, through Lucy's deliberate self-abasement, the depth of her compassionate response to Reardon's suffering.

IV *The Holy Rollers*

There is a third section of action in *Strange Children* that seems, on first reading, to be only remotely, and perhaps somewhat arbitrarily, related to the other two more tightly interwoven actions. This part has to do with the MacDonoughs, the family of poor-white tenants on the Lewis farm. The MacDonoughs and their friends who are Holy Rollers, have fixed on one verse of the Bible and made it the basis of their religion: "They shall take up serpents; and if they drink any deadly thing, it shall not hurt them."[14] The founder of this sect had interpreted these words to mean that he must take up snakes; at revival meetings he would hold a rattlesnake and even allow it to coil about his neck as a sign of his faith. Yet, when he was thirty-six, he had been bitten by a young rattler and died. He was buried in the Lewis' woods and "is still regarded as a martyr by the faithful."[15] The MacDonoughs are among the faithful; and, as the novel opens, the Holy Rollers are preparing to hold a revival meeting at a brush arbor they are constructing beneath the hill on which the Lewis house sits. During dinner the evening of the Reardons' arrival when the Lewises and their guest are chattering in a brittle way about Kevin Reardon's pious old father, the words and the music of a primitive hymn being sung by the Holy Rollers drifts in through the open windows. Uncle Tubby is amused, of course, and makes what he regards as clever remarks not only about the crudeness of the Holy Rollers in particular but about religious faith in general. Of the guests, only

Kevin Reardon is seriously interested in knowing the details of the theology of the Holy Rollers.

Miss Gordon introduces the Holy Rollers for a number of reasons. In the first place, they are interesting in themselves; secondly, the MacDonough tenants on the Lewis farm help lend the novel solidity: we see them not only in their revival meeting but also as they perform their chores and as Mrs. MacDonough nurses her baby. More important, though, their solid presence is a counterweight to the otherworld atmosphere created by the Reardons and Uncle Tubby. The MacDonoughs are ignorant, unsophisticated, and physically unattractive people; but the father and mother are both unambitious for the material things of this world, and they are also people of deep religious faith. Like Kevin Reardon, Mrs. MacDonough has had mystical experiences: she has seen Jesus flying about her house on a broom and has spoken in the "Unknown Tongue," which is "The proof that you have received the Gift of the Spirit."[16] Mr. MacDonough contrasts to Stephen Lewis, who, like Jim Chapman, is a paralyzed intellectual. Both a selfless man and a man of faith, MacDonough is not interested in using others for his own gain—he wants to see them saved—and he demonstrates his faith by picking up a rattlesnake at the revival meeting.

The world of the MacDonoughs also functions in the novel as a way of commenting on the other actions. The story of Isabel, of Kevin Reardon and Uncle Tubby, of Lucy and her parents, and of the Holy Rollers is brought together at the end of the novel. Almost at the precise moment that Mr. MacDonough is bitten by the rattler, it is discovered that Isabel and Tubby have eloped. Lucy returns the crucifix to Reardon who is all but crushed at the news of his wife's desertion and of his friend's treachery. On the final page of the novel, Lucy's father raises the meaning of these actions to a higher level of significance: "He told himself that it would have been no great matter if that man [MacDonough] had died tonight, for all men, it appeared to him now, for the first time, die on the same day: the day on which their appointed task is finished. If that man had made his last journey tonight he would not have gone alone, but accompanied by a larger presence, as the friend standing behind him had been companioned when he, too, lay at the point of death, in a strange country and in a desert."[17]

Thus *Strange Children* has been, on its highest level, a novel about evil and about the necessity, for those who would escape it, of religious faith. Evil—call it what you will—has existed in all places and in all times and is committed by those who are blind to the deepest fact of religious truth—that temporal life is nothing; eternal life, everything. Only those who are reborn are saved from final destruction. However, Miss Gordon does not state her meaning this directly. To do so would be inartistic and, for most readers, unconvincing. She makes her point indirectly and negatively through Stephen Lewis who is not a Christian but a learned man who sees the truth but cannot experience it. All he can feel in the presence of this insight is the terrible anguish of its deprivation: "He saw that those days, those years had been moving toward this moment and he wondered what moment was being prepared for him and for his wife and his child, and he groaned, so loud that the woman and the child stared at him, wondering, too."[18]

CHAPTER 10

A Christian Comedy

The Malefactors (1956), Caroline Gordon's next and as of this writing her last novel,[1] begins where *The Strange Children* left off; the protagonist of this second "Catholic" novel is in much the same position spiritually that Stephen Lewis was at the end of *The Strange Children*—he is in need of religious faith but unable to believe. There is, however, an important difference: Stephen Lewis is aware of his deficiency; Thomas Claiborne, protagonist of *The Malefactors*, is not, at least not at the beginning of the novel. Indeed, *The Malefactors* is the story of Claiborne's spiritual awakening and of his eventual religious conversion.

I *The Issue*

As the novel opens, Thomas Claiborne is at breakfast on the terrace of his wife's rural home in Bucks County, Pennsylvania. Claiborne is a poet or, more properly, he is a forty-eight-year-old man of letters who once wrote poetry but who now merely goes through the motions of writing. Each day he locks himself away in his study and pretends to his wife that he is working on a long poem. Actually, he does little more than lie on a couch and let his erudite mind wander. Indeed, things have come to such a pass that Claiborne has begun to carry on a dialogue with himself, or rather with a "voice" inside his head that makes critical comments about his behavior and state of mind.

As Claiborne sits staring out over the carefully manicured lawn, his wife Vera comes suddenly around the house leading her prize bull. Vera is a rich woman with a passion for farming and for raising red poll cattle, and this is the day of a festival she is having to show her prize bull, Bud. To Vera's festival come Molly Archer, a rich widow recently remarried; her new husband Ed, the editor of a big circulation magazine; George Crenfew, a psychiatrist and Claiborne's first cousin; Crenfew's wife Marcia, a psychologist with a penchant for seeing life in terms of sexual perversion; Max Shull, a painter who knew the Claibornes years before when they were living in Paris and who is now existing on Vera's bounty. There are also a number of "natives": Joe Hess, a farmer, who is enthusiastic about artificial insemination in cattle, and Ed Applekeller, a Dunkard, who is just as strongly opposed to it. In addition, there are two women visitors from the "outside world": Cynthia Vail, a cousin of Vera who has left her husband in Wisconsin and who has gone East to establish a career as a poet, and Catherine Pollard, who was George Crenfew's first wife and who now runs a Catholic hostel for social outcasts in the slums of New York.

Among the gaily decorated stands and stalls of Vera's festival, Tom Claiborne, superior and detached, moves with a whisky in his hand. Of the guests, only two people engage his interest: Vera's cousin Cynthia Vail and Catherine Pollard, who has come from New York for Vera's festival. The attraction that these women exert on Claiborne is of a very different order. Cynthia exacts from Claiborne a sense of obligation for something that happened in the past—she makes him feel that he owes her something. Catherine Pollard, on the other hand, fills Claiborne with a "curious lightness of heart," and he cannot "rid himself of the impression that they had agreed to travel together to . . . a goal so splendid that he had glimpsed it only in dreams. . . ."[2] But Claiborne is not ready to make that journey yet, for he has not learned what it means to suffer.

In time, he learns; and Cynthia Vail, Vera's cousin, teaches him. At first, as Claiborne becomes interested in Cynthia, he feels, or imagines he feels, a resurgence of his old creative powers. He takes Cynthia as his mistress and breaks with Vera. Then he assumes the editorship of a large-circulation literary magazine, which is for him a kind of artistic prostitution. Cynthia persuades him to "borrow" two very elegant apartments belonging to a literary "lion hunter" and her invalid husband. At first, Claiborne resists, but after some pressure from Cynthia, he acquiesces. For a time, he conceals from Vera his affair with Cynthia; then, because of an argument with Marcia Crenfew, the Freudian psychologist, his infidelity is exposed. Vera forgives him, but Claiborne leaves her for Cynthia. Vera tries to commit suicide but is prevented by her brother, Robin. When Claiborne hears of Vera's attempt to kill herself, he is deeply upset; but since he is still unaware of the suffering that pushed Vera to such an extreme, he makes no real effort to see her.

The next day at his office Claiborne reads a letter from Catherine Pollard asking him to come to her hostel on Mott Street in the Bowery to talk to a nun who is writing a book about Horne Watts, a talented but perverted young poet whom Claiborne had known years before. When Claiborne almost against his will goes to see the nun, his visit marks the beginning of the change in his life. The nun, Sister Immaculata, tells him that Horne Watts's homosexuality and impassioned frenzy were attempts to find God. Claiborne rejects most of what the nun tells him about Watts, and he also refuses her invitation to pray for "our boy."

That same evening at a party that he and Cynthia stage in the borrowed apartments, Claiborne begins to realize the extent to which he has sunk morally. He is humiliated, first of all, by the falseness of his and Cynthia's situation and, second, by the presence of several of the guests who have come to see the "love nest" or to fulfill their sense of obligation. He also begins to feel the corruption implicit in his possession of these lavish apartments, but what really opens Claiborne's eyes is a quarrel with Cynthia over his behavior at the party. Cynthia says he spoiled the party by offending a rich and important guest who might withdraw money from a project in which she is interested. In his argument with Cynthia, Claiborne is forced to recognize that Cynthia is without feelings or principles that are unrelated to her own self-advancement; he is also made aware that, whatever Vera's faults, she is "at least a woman."[3]

That night, after his quarrel with Cynthia, Claiborne has a nightmare that is so horrifying it sends him fleeing to his good friend and cousin George Crenfew, who happens also to be a psychiatrist. Crenfew's analysis of Claiborne's dream makes him realize things about himself and about his father, whom he hates, that he had not known before; but the interview solves nothing, first, because Claiborne is still not prepared to face the truth about himself and, second, because psychotherapy is not the road marked out for his recovery. After Claiborne has left Crenfew's office and has gone home, he sees, while in a drunken state of mental clarity, the truth: Vera is the only one in the world who does not judge him and the reason, of course, is that she loves him.

This insight is the product of Claiborne's own suffering, and it moves him to act. Unshaven, and in clothing so wrinkled that he is easily mistaken for a bum, Clairborne goes in search of Vera. He finds her on Catherine Pollard's farm for social derelicts, tending a senile old man and a dumb child. A priest whom Claiborne encounters there tells him to remember that a wife is as subject to her husband as the Church is to Christ, but Claiborne in his fallen state is unable to assert any mastery over Vera. Instead, he quarrels with her and races madly back to New York City.

Alone in his apartment that night, Claiborne has another vivid dream in which Horne Watts appears and leads him to Catherine Pollard. The next morning Claiborne rushes off to see Catherine, bearing a small bouquet of flowers. He finds her in the chapel of her hostel on Mott Street. During their talk, Catherine tells him something that makes it possible for him to go back to Vera. When she was a small child, Vera was baptized Catholic. The knowledge that Vera is in the Church and therefore subject to its laws gives Claiborne the courage to assert his mastery over her. It also produces in him the first signs of genuine humility. He thinks, as he is driving back to the farm to see Vera again, that, if there is no bed for him there, he can sleep in the hay. And then this sentence brings the book to its close: "He could be sitting there on the bench with *the other bums* when she came down in the morning."[4] This desired reunion with Vera and the calm sense of his own unworthiness evidently signify Claiborne's religious conversion.

II *The Technique*

The Malefactors is clearly Caroline Gordon's most ambitious, most complex, and technically her most accomplished long work. Her handling of Claiborne's central intelligence point of view is so masterful that we immediately recall Henry James's *The Ambassadors*, which has obviously been an influence on this novel. However, Thomas Claiborne's intelligence and the nature of his discovery are quite different from that of Lambert Strether. Strether's revelation comes almost entirely because of outer events; Claiborne's in large part because of changes going on within him. Claiborne learns, as does Strether, during the course of the action; but the change that takes place in him is deeper and of more significance than that which occurs in James's hero. I do not imply, of course, that *The Malefactors* is better than *The Ambassadors*, but only that it is, because of certain technical resemblances, a similar kind of novel.

Another impressive technical accomplishment in *The Malefactors* is the way Miss Gordon abandons, to some extent, straightforward chronology in favor of a more poetic compositional method. There is a plot, but it has been so flattened and interspersed with bits and pieces from the past and with seemingly irrelevant scenes in the present that we are not often aware that a story is being told. There is, of course, a loss in this method; but there are also advantages: by telling her story this way, Miss Gordon is able to juxtapose characters and events that could not be related by a more conventional temporal narrative structure. For example, a sequence of three scenes toward the middle of the book appears to have no significant relationship. In the first scene, Claiborne encounters his wife hulling walnuts under a tree; in the second, he is in his Aunt Virginia's bedroom; in the third he is on his way to see his mistress again and encounters Vera still seated beneath the tree hulling walnuts. The scene that takes place in Virginia Claiborne's bedroom appears to have no meaningful connection to what came before or to what is about to happen. Claiborne and his aunt merely talked about Eupedon, the family estate in Kentucky which was flooded to make way for a vast power project. Aunt Virginia tells a sentimental anecdote about how she "first learned about Santa Claus" and about how kind Claiborne's father was to "children and niggers." There are reminiscences about the walnut trees at Eupedon, and Aunt Virginia bitterly laments the loss of those trees and of the family estate that is now under water. The scene closes as Aunt Virginia tells Claiborne: "After all, it's something to be a Claiborne. I hope you'll never forget that, Tom."[5]

Except as possible background material about Claiborne's origins, this scene, as we read it, seems pointless; but as we begin the next chapter with its opening sentence ("Vera was still sitting on the ground under the beech tree hulling walnuts."),[6] the events of this scene and the one before it are suddenly thrown into perspective. Connections are also established between the details and characters of this scene in Aunt Virginia's bedroom and other sections of the novel. We are made to feel, for example, the essential difference between Claiborne's aunt and his wife. His aunt is preoccupied with the past, with sentimental tales about herself and with the fictitious value of the Claiborne name. Vera, whatever her limitations of talent and intellect (she neither writes nor thinks deep thoughts), is alive; for whether she lives in the Auvergne in France or Bucks County, Pennsylvania, she enjoys life and takes pleasure in gardening, in tending cattle, or in crushing the hulls of walnuts.

Moreover, certain details in that first scene, which takes place before Claiborne goes to his aunt's bedroom and which included what seemed merely gratuitous details about Tom's father, are now charged with significance. As Claiborne's nostrils sting with the odor that in boyhood had been so familiar (the smell of crushed walnut hulls), he remembers fall at Eupedon and the three great walnut trees that stood beside the smokehouse; and this memory causes him to recollect the way the walnuts were collected into piles between the kitchen and the outkitchen, and how his father liked to sit in a low, split-bottom chair beside the heap and hull walnuts with a hammer just the way Vera was doing now. His father had said on one occasion that walnuts smelled like fall: "I always think they smell more like fall than anything."[7] What we see vividly is that the picture Claiborne has already given us of his father as a "dark histrionic man too lazy and indifferent to practice any profession but whoring and gambling," is wrong.[8] We realize now that, whatever Claiborne's father's faults, he was at least alive to the simple natural pleasures of the world; we recognize after some reflection that the elder Claiborne's faults were the result perhaps of too much passion for life. We are made aware by this sudden illuminating detail that, despite his dislike of his aunt, who bores him, Claiborne is very much like her. He too is an invalid. He too has cut himself off from the natural world and retreated into a world that is artificial, intellectual, and sterile.

The scene just analyzed is also related to at least two other scenes: one that takes place earlier in this same bedroom and a later one that occurs in the lavish apartment borrowed from the Brodos by Claiborne. In the first scene, Catherine Pollard fills the sick room with lively talk and with a sense of life that makes us aware of Virginia Claiborne's bloodlessness. In the second scene, Claiborne is lying in the hospital bed that has been disguised to look like a medieval antique. This scene links him with the paralyzed rich owner, whose malady has been concealed from the outside world by his money and to his aunt, who simply went to bed because living was too much for her.

The technique of *The Malefactors* is impressive not only because Miss Gordon has accomplished something that is difficult to do but, more important, because the technique is beautifully suited to the story she is telling. Indeed, without this technique—the special combination of the central intelligence with the juxta-positioning and patterning of motifs—the story of Thomas Cren-few Claiborne could only have ended ironically. As it is, however, Miss Gordon has managed to accommodate both Claiborne's "Waste Land" vision and Vera's Christian one by allowing

Claiborne's to dominate during the early chapters of the novel
while having the other gradually assume dominance.

In generalizing about her method, I have, of course, over-
simplified; we are never quite aware of these visions as such. They
are suggested, or, if made explicit, they come from the point of
view of a character such as Sister Immaculata or Father Emmet
to whom we have a neutral response. There is, however, one
character who does more to establish the dominance of the Christian point of view than anyone else in the novel—Catherine Pollard, who is something of a saint. Miss Gordon suggests this
saintliness in a number of different ways, chiefly by letting us see
the kind of person she is now and what she used to be. When
Claiborne knew her years before in Paris, she was a drunken,
irresponsible young woman married to his cousin George Crenfew.
Even in that condition Catherine was able to see that there was
nothing she could do to save her marriage. She left her husband
and child and entered the Church. When Claiborne meets her
again at his wife's festival in Pennsylvania, Catherine is a kind
of Catholic lay sister running a hostel in the Bowery. Catherine
Pollard has not taken this job because she feels she ought to: she
has taken it out of boundless love for the outcasts who stumble in
from the streets.

Though Catherine Pollard has become a serious and responsible
woman, she is neither solemn nor otherworldly. She has a marvelous
laugh and a keen sense of humor; and, like Vera, she takes delight
in the simple pleasures of this world. Claiborne is immediately
drawn to her, though the company of everyone else bores him. The
attraction Claiborne feels for Catherine Pollard is a sign of his
unconscious attraction to the religious life which he cannot admit
to or even realize during much of the novel. As the action moves
toward its close, this attraction becomes so strong that Catherine
Pollard appears in Claiborne's dream and is eventually responsible
for leading him into the Church. The reason for this increasing
power of Catherine Pollard is then revealed. As soon as she had
heard about his and Vera's difficulties, she had begun praying for
him.

In making Claiborne's change of character depend so heavily
on a supernatural explanation, Miss Gordon is aware that she is
taking leave of realistic conventions. She does not, however, insist
that Catherine Pollard's prayers have wrought this change; she
merely presents the facts and lets us make the generalizations for
ourselves. Also, as another important way of making Claiborne's

conversion convincing, she uses a technique employed in her earlier novels, the historical paradigm, but the paradigms now come from Catholic history. The most important of these religious paradigms is St. Eustace, a Roman general who was converted when the stag he was hunting turned at bay and he saw Christ hanging on the cross between its horns.[9] He then "refused to sacrifice to the pagan gods so they threw him and his family to the lions . . . who lay down and licked their feet." Then St. Eustace and his family were imprisoned in a bull made of brass and burnt to death.[10]

The connection between St. Eustace and the characters in *The Malefactors* is established in several ways. There is, first of all, Vera's bull who might be said to symbolize the masculine principle in its purely natural state. What Bud, the bull, does depends in large part on whether he is controlled and used by man. Blind, uncontrolled masculine power, if unchecked by humility and love, is deadly and destructive. For a time, it appears that Claiborne himself will cast his lot with those of this world who might be said to be worshippers of pagan gods and modern minotaurs. This possibility is suggested overtly by Claiborne's attitude toward Vera's bull. When the bull gets into the Hess's pasture where two heifers are grazing and, in the neighbor's view, spoils them, Claiborne comments to himself, "a bull raping a heifer. . . . But what are bulls—and heifers—for?"[11] The use of the word *rape* makes the point; for, by using it, Claiborne puts himself in the same category of those for whom mating is not a natural act but one of violence. But it is in his own behavior that Claiborne most fully aligns himself with the forces of violence. In a moment of drunkenness, he seduces Cynthia Vail (who, it turns out later, has led him on); and, through her, he finds himself increasingly aligned with those who worship the twin gods of contemporary paganism: fame and money.

The explicit connection between St. Eustace and Claiborne is made by Max Shull, a painter who lives with the Claibornes. Shull, who had painted St. Eustace and the stag many years ago, is now, under the encouragement of Catherine Pollard, working on a mural for her chapel. Though Max has failed conspicuously as a painter, even Claiborne is amazed at the power of this mural. Also, Max's painting has managed to attract the interest of a number of young people, including Vera's bachelor brother Robin and George Crenfew's homely daughter Désirée; and it gives both of them something in this world worth devoting themselves to.

In addition to the paradigm of St. Eustace, Miss Gordon also depends upon the example of St. Catherine of Siena and her friend Blessed Ramon.[12] The reference to St. Catherine is made by the nun, Sister Immaculata, who has discovered significant connections between the blood imagery in St. Catherine's writing and that in the poetry of Horne Watts.[13] Sister Immaculata has discovered that Horne Watts and Catherine Pollard before her conversion were experimenting with magic that they believed would enable them to witness the creation of the universe in a mixture of consecrated wine and water. Despite Watts's well-known depravities, Sister Immaculata thinks that Watts was close to a religious conversion at the time of his suicide. Since Watts's death, Catherine Pollard has prayed for his soul; and, judging from the fact that it is Watts who appears in Claiborne's dream and leads him to Catherine Pollard, it seems that her prayers have been efficacious.

The connection between Horne Watts and Thomas Claiborne is also significant in the development of Claiborne's conversion. Claiborne thought highly of Watts's poetry but he felt superior to him because of his lack of formal education, his alcoholism, and his homosexuality. What the reader sees is that Claiborne himself is becoming an alcoholic and that, like Watts, his poetic power has faded. Moreover, though he is not homosexual, his affair with Cynthia Vail is a kind of perversion. Like Horne Watts, Claiborne also moves to the brink of suicide. The parallels linking St. Catherine of Siena and Blessed Ramon to Catherine Pollard and Horne Watts and then, later, Catherine Pollard to Thomas Claiborne function like motifs—they are not meant to convince through cause and effect but to lead the reader to make the connections for himself: If a saintly woman named Catherine can influence the life of a poet in Italy in the fourteenth century, why cannot a saintly woman named Catherine in 1956 influence a poet in New York City?

Miss Gordon's paradigms from religious history are reinforced by others from contemporary life, including persons who are still alive. Horne Watts is certainly based on Hart Crane with whom the Tates were closely associated in the 1920's and 1930's. Catherine Pollard is evidently modeled on Dorothy Day, who still operates a Catholic mission in the Bowery district of New York City.[14] The Claibornes are clearly based on Caroline Gordon and Allen Tate. Carlo Vincent, Vera's eccentric father, was suggested apparently by the equally eccentric Italian painter Giorgio de Chirico.[15] And there are doubtless a number of other characters in this novel who have been based on actual persons. The question naturally arises: what is the point of these parallels? How is the reader to respond to them? One critic who has found them a source of "constant embarrassment," concludes that *The Malefactors* "takes on the nature of a public confessional."[16]

It is, of course, impossible to predict how every reader will respond to such apparently autobiographical references, but there is no good reason why critics should be disconcerted by *The Malefactors*. It is not even a very autobiographical novel, for Miss Gordon has simply availed herself of the large facts from the lives of her contemporary paradigms and has invoked these as she has historical paradigms and for much the same reasons. They are her "proofs" that, contrary to modern prejudice against mystical experiences, the things she has happen in her novels can happen. Indeed, since they have happened, Miss Gordon depends upon this factual authority to help give her fiction credibility. In order to convince rather than to confess Miss Gordon has invoked familiar figures from the present and from the recent past. Thomas Claiborne's first meeting with Catherine Pollard occurs early in the novel, and at that time he feels mysteriously drawn to travel somewhere with her.[17] But not until the close of the book do Claiborne and Catherine meet again and is Claiborne finally ready to accompany her on that journey. There are at least two significant reasons for this long delay. First, Claiborne must suffer and learn what that journey means. The second reason—and it is in large part a matter of fictional strategy—is that Claiborne and Catherine Pollard must be kept apart until both the need for and the meaning of that journey can be established. Indeed, we might conclude that almost everything that lies between Claiborne's two meetings with Catherine Pollard exists primarily to establish these two objectives.

III *Religious Questionings*

In order to make the reader feel the need, even the necessity, for Claiborne to find the true way, Miss Gordon has also to meet and to answer the doubts that many readers are likely to have. The most important of these is the common view that religious mysticism necessarily means a lack of concern for the welfare of others. Another is the belief that the need for religious faith is a sign of weakness. The first question is raised implicitly in the contrast established between Virginia Claiborne, Tom Claiborne's aunt, and Catherine Pollard. When Virginia Claiborne was young, she had joined the Methodist Church and worked in the Epworth League. Her interest in the church was merely social, for there was nothing else at the time for an unmarriageable young woman to do. As soon as she moved to the city, Virginia's interest shifted to the study of law; and she passed the bar examinations and practiced law for ten years. Then she gave that up for the more comfortable life of an invalid. Catherine Pollard, on the other hand, went into the Catholic Church because she was earnestly, passionately seeking God. When she had found what she was looking for, she did not settle into self-complacency; she devoted her life to "being Christ" to her fellow man.[18] Joining the church, then, does not mean a selfish preoccupation with the saving of her own soul. Personal problems may lead one into the Church; but, after one has crossed that threshold and is himself secure, he has an opportunity to assist others.

Another attitude Miss Gordon appears to be challenging in this novel is the commonly heard complaint that religion is a crutch for the man or woman who cannot solve his own problems. This criticism is implicitly answered in the contrast between Virginia Claiborne and Catherine Pollard, and it is pointedly attacked in the parallels and contrasts between Max Shull, the failed painter who lives on Vera's farm, and Horne Watts, the young poet who committed suicide. Shull is still living, getting a little fat, and puttering around with his paints. Watts, on the other hand, enjoyed a brief but hectic career as a poet. In the middle of his life, he threw himself from the deck of a steamer into the sea. Miss Gordon makes it clear that, while there are some obvious similarities between Horne Watts and Max Shull (both artists, both homosexuals), there are also some crucial differences. Shull enjoys his effeminacy, whereas Watts rejected his and tried to be masculine. Moreover, Horne Watts was filled with "passionate intensity," not for himself, but for life, for man, and ultimately for God. The point Miss Gordon is making in the parallels between Shull and Watts is stated by Sister Immaculata who quotes Christ: "Some men are born eunuchs, some men are made eunuchs by men and some become eunuchs for the sake of the Kingdom of God."[19] A religious conversion, contrary to the popular view, can be a heroic struggle that involves self-discipline and self-sacrifice; whereas living outside the church can mean, as Max Shull illustrates, a pitiful weakness.

IV   The Meaning of Sex

There is in *The Malefactors* a great deal of emphasis upon sex, particularly upon sexual perversions, a fact which surprised Miss Gordon herself when it came to her attention; for, as she remarked, she does not usually deal with such matters.[20] In a novel such as *The Malefactors*, however, which attempts to grapple with the anti-religious bent of our times, attitudes toward sex, particularly the question of sexual perversion, have to be dealt with. Miss Gordon has Claiborne remark of Marcia Crenfew's Freudianism—a remark that could be applied generally to these times—"You've got it turned upside down."[21] In other words, what passes for love in our society is, at best, sex, and, at its worst, often perversion; and what is called perversion (or "sexual maladjustment") is often love, sometimes love of the highest order. The problem of sex is, therefore, deeply involved in the more general question about whether religion is a retreat from reality.

Miss Gordon has made it clear both in print and out that she does not approve of homosexuality.[22] In *The Malefactors*, she puts that vice in perspective as one of many human vices. For some, vice is drink; for others, lechery, greed, or unfettered ambition. There is also that modern vice, the desire to reduce all human relationships to the mechanics of sex. The desire to mechanize love and the passion for money, Miss Gordon sees as intimately related. She dramatizes this connection in a scene that takes place during Vera's festival. A young man in a white refrigerated truck appears dressed in the white garb of the medical scientist. He is the representative of a company specializing in artificial insemination, and he delivers a spiel to Vera's guests about the advantages in cattle breeding of artificial insemination. The young man spouts the jargon of science, but what he is really doing, of course, is delivering a sales pitch for his product. All of the advantages this salesman gives relate to but one argument—money.

The objections against artificial insemination are put into the mouth of an old Dunkard, Ed Applekeller, who is also a shrewd farmer: "*As a beast of the field I am with Thee all the day*. The cattle was put here for a picture of ourselves. It's up to us to guide 'em and use 'em, the way the Lord does us, but only according to what's right . . . [artificial insemination] is against nature. Cattle have got their nature same as a man's got his nature. It's up to a man to respect it."[23] Vera too is outraged by such cruelty perpetrated on dumb animals, but Claiborne is only amused. He is, as we have seen, also amused when Vera's prize bull gets into a neighbor's pasture and "rapes" two cows. Miss Gordon's point is that the mating of animals is part of the natural order, but it is not what animals are "for" any more than rape is what women are for. To say otherwise is to embrace what is ultimately a perverted view of life.

Despite Claiborne's refusal to take seriously Vera's objections to artificial insemination or to regard the sexual problems of animals with anything but a cynical view, Claiborne himself takes violent exception to certain intellectual perversions of man's sexual nature. The chief practitioner of this cult is George Crenfew's second wife, Marcia, a small, chinless woman who takes satisfaction in reducing the complexities of art and life to Freudian simplicities. For example, when Marcia and Claiborne are looking at a piece of sculpture constructed out of junk by Vera's brother Robin, an overaged bachelor, Marcia makes an asinine comment on Robin's sculpture: "Interesting isn't it that he puts such a limitation on himself? Makes the phallic concentration all the more obvious."[24] In another work of art, this time a painting of a religious subject by Max Shull, Marcia finds the whole sad story of the painter's homosexuality. When Claiborne tells her that the title of the painting is *The Vision of St. Eustace* and that the erection between the horns of the bull is a cross and not a phallus, Marcia smiles. "Can't the cross be a phallic symbol?" she inquires sweetly.[25] At this point, Claiborne loses control of himself and makes what is clearly the author's own view of a common attitude toward religion and sex. "*No! No!*" Claiborne cries. "She's got it upside down: They stood her on her head twenty years ago and she's never got right side up. It wouldn't be so bad if she was the only one, but we've got factories turning her out by the hundreds."[26]

Claiborne's deep emotional opposition to Marcia's perverted vision is pictured even more forcefully in an argument he has with her several days later while on a commuter train going into New York City. On this occasion Marcia has managed to turn Baudelaire's great poem *Le Rêve Parisien* into the manifestations of a trauma suffered by the poet when he discovered his parents "in coitus." "If you were my wife," he tells her, "I'd hang you up by your heels till all the crap drained out of you—if it took the rest of your life."[27] The point of this scene, though it is not made explicitly, is that Marcia Crenfew has a typically modern but incorrect view of art. Whatever trauma Baudelaire may have suffered, his art, particularly the stanzas quoted by Marcia, arises from much deeper levels of the mind than she is aware of. Baudelaire's poetry, like all great art, springs from the soul and expresses, in images drawn from the unconscious, universal truths.

V *Sex and the Main Plot*

Though Claiborne is gifted with a poet's vision, he lacks the ability to keep himself from falling into the chasm that yawns at his feet and at those of every mortal: he allows himself to be seduced by Cynthia Vail. The affair of Claiborne and Cynthia develops on a somewhat higher level some of the same points Miss Gordon has been making in the sections of the novel dealing with natural mating, with artificial insemination, and with homosexual and Freudian perversion. According to standards rather widely held in our society, there is nothing at all unnatural in the affair of Claiborne and Cynthia Vail. He is tired of his wife; she of her husband. She is attracted to Claiborne; he, to her. Why shouldn't they then sleep together?

Miss Gordon, of course, does not deal with the question of uninhibited sexual experiences in such general terms. She is concerned with two specific people and with certain specific backgrounds, attitudes, and characters; but what she says about this relationship has applicability to human conduct generally. The fault to be found with this relationship is quite simply that it is not founded on love. Claiborne's attraction to Cynthia is a product of lust and pride; for, after all, Cynthia admires and looks up to Claiborne as a great poet. Vera does not worship Claiborne's public image; she loves him. Because Cynthia does not love him (she does not apparently love anyone but herself), she makes no demands on him; she liberates him in a curious way from the ties that bind most men to their fellow creatures. Like all of Miss Gordon's villains, Cynthia has no standards, no code of conduct, no theory of life except her own ambitions. As a consequence, she does not hesitate to take the most convenient view of everyone she knows. Cynthia's cynicism makes Claiborne feel that he has joined her on a strange quest (one very different from the light-hearted journey promised by Catherine Pollard), "in some vast cavern underground, their only light the torch which played now on this marmoreal figure, now on that, figures whose pose, whose features seemed at first glance familiar but which in the gleam of the torch held up in her frail hand, would suddenly lean forward in an attitude never assumed in life, emit from under shadowy brows looks never leveled on fellow mortals."[28]

On Cynthia's part (we don't see her fully since everything in the novel comes through Claiborne's point of view), the relationship is strictly one of convenience and usefulness. Since Cynthia wants to be a good poet and to publish in important places, Claiborne, a good poet and still a fine critic, can open important doors for her. She gives him her body in return for the favors he can do for her; and, when she is through with him, she moves to another man who has more money and who is in a position to back her publishing schemes. For Cynthia, in other words, the relationship with Claiborne is simply a form of prostitution and therefore a perversion.

For Claiborne, the affair with Cynthia is a form of self-indulgence, self-deception, and evasion. He has turned his back on Vera because she demands something from him that is difficult, almost impossible, for him to give—himself. This limitation is something that, in the course of the novel, Claiborne finally recognizes. When he has accepted that knowledge, he is then faced with the very difficult task of giving himself to Vera. And his is not, Miss Gordon shows, a slavish devotion; on the contrary, it requires, first of all, that he become master in his own house and learn to impose his will with wisdom.

VI *Claiborne's Choice*

If Vera may be said to represent the true way for Claiborne, Cynthia Vail represents the false way. Miss Gordon reinforces the choices represented by Vera and Cynthia by associating Vera with the sun and Cynthia with the moon. Vera is usually outside in the fields or in the midst of some homely activity such as caring for her cattle or arranging for her festival. Her affection for Claiborne is offered in the open daylight. Cynthia's first covert advance to Claiborne is made on a moonlit night when she lays a hand on his arm, and Claiborne "could feel its chill through his thin coatsleeve. A drop of water fell on the gravel between them. He put his own hand up and laid it for a second over her cold hand, then looked up to see where the moon had gone."[29] Their first embrace takes place in a cave several feet underground, and Cynthia's influence over Claiborne is likened, as we have seen, to a journey through dark caverns lighted only by a torch carried in her frail hand.

This exotic imagery is the author's way of suggesting that what Cynthia offers to Claiborne is not love and natural affection but a subterranean existence beautiful with a borrowed elegance that is coldly calculated to achieve its effect—to make Cynthia Vail appear in the best possible light and, consequently, to help her rise in the literary world. In contrast, when Vera offers Claiborne herself, all she asks in return is his love. Vera's demand on Claiborne is, of course, almost more than he can bear; for Claiborne himself lives in the underground world where Cynthia is too much at home. When Cynthia smiles on him and takes him into her confidence by laying bare some of the sordid details about her own and Vera's family, Claiborne is delighted; for he has never before known a woman who was less inhibited by the rules with which most people govern their lives. Vera never gossips about her family and never judges her father's eccentric behavior, but Cynthia unabashedly tells Claiborne that her mother divorced her father in order to marry a man with money. She also reveals to Claiborne secrets about Vera's family, particularly about her father's last years, his narcissism and his suicide.

Vera's father, Carlo Vincent, or Vencenzzi as his name was before he anglicized it, is closely related thematically to both Cynthia and Claiborne. Cynthia clearly shares her uncle's preoccupation with self; but Claiborne, who detests Carlo's painting, also resembles him. For Claiborne too is absorbed with himself, or as his "voice" tells him when he asks himself whether Vera will come back to him: *"There isn't anything to go back to—except that circle that long ago you described and then of your own free will stepped inside, keeping it inviolate by flailing down any living thing that sprang up in it, so that there should be left in it nothing but yourself and the air that goes in and out of your rotting lungs. Would a woman want to step again inside that circle, breathe again that impoverished air?"*[30]

Claiborne's absorption is heavily underscored by the major technique of the novel, the device of the central intelligence which permits us to see everything through his eyes. His preoccupation with himself also appears directly in his blindness to Vera's feeling for him, in his ability to love or to think well of other people ("I hate my fellow men," he tells Vera,)[31] in his frequent conversations with his inner voice, and even in his affair with Cynthia (for in her admiration of his poetic judgment she is but a reflection of him)—all of these are manifestations of Claiborne's ingrown sensibility. The dangers that lie open before him are dramatized by the several dreams in which he finds himself running in company with Carlo Vincent and Horne Watts, both of whom were alcoholic, homosexual, and ultimately suicides.

Though Claiborne's dream would be given a Freudian reading by Marcia Crenfew and though Claiborne himself thinks of its purely sexual implications, Miss Gordon supplies another meaning. She has George Crenfew say of one dream, that it is perhaps a warning to Claiborne of what could happen to him unless he alters his course, for he too is heading toward self-destruction. Significantly, Horne Watts, who fought heroically to escape the prison of his flesh, appears in Claiborne's final dream and leads him to Catherine Pollard, who exemplifies the highest kind of love of which man is capable. And it is Catherine Pollard, as we have seen, who points out to Claiborne the way to save himself.

VII *Conclusion*

This account of Tom Claiborne's salvation through reunion with his wife resembles Jim Chapman's reconciliation with his wife in *Women on the Porch*, but with the important difference that the whole tradition of Catholic belief has now provided a basis for the reconciliation. The meaning of Claiborne's reunion with Vera is not just that he has been saved from the hell of his paralyzed conditions but that he has also been redeemed from the hell of Christian myth. This meaning will not be enthusiastically received by skeptical critics, but it is one that can hardly be ignored in any serious readings of the novel. Unlike some Catholic writers, notably J. F. Powers and Flannery O'Connor, who approach their faith through ambiguities and negations, Miss Gordon is quite direct;[32] indeed, her indirections are deliberate fictional strategies and not emotional ambiguities.

The Malefactors was probably not written as an answer to those for whom the meaninglessness of existence is the main truth, rather than the chief myth of our age; but to read it in this light adds to our understanding of this novel. Miss Gordon's early fiction, as we have seen, would have no part of this myth. The fictional worlds created in her novels were dominated by those who acted, either for themselves or in the name of an ideal. There were no paralyzed, suffering heroes; when there was suffering, it was presented as something to be endured as part of man's inevitable lot. The protagonists of these novels were old-fashioned heroes, identified with some remote time and culture. *The Male-*

factors, like *Women on the Porch* and *Strange Children*, takes on the modern myth, admits that fear and paralysis are possible attributes of a fictional protagonist, but insists that a hero must still oppose the enemy—in this case, the hero's own darker self. Miss Gordon's religious commitments also make it possible, perhaps demand, that her new hero have with him a "large presence" to lift and sustain him on his perilous journey through life.

CHAPTER 11

Art and Theme in the Short Story

"I AM not a short story writer," Caroline Gordon has asserted; "I am a novelist."[1] And the facts would seem to bear her out. In the forty or so years that she has been writing fiction, Miss Gordon has published eight novels and only two collections of short stories. The first, *The Forest of the South* (1945), contains seventeen stories published over a period of sixteen years. The second, *Old Red and Other Stories* (1963), contains thirteen pieces, nine of which appeared in the earlier collection. Altogether, Miss Gordon has published during her career in book form twenty-one stories, enough to fill one volume the length of one of her longer novels. And yet, curiously, she is better known as a short-story writer than as a novelist. Two of her best-known stories are "The Captive" and "Old Red"; three other short stories also appear frequently in anthologies of modern fiction: "The Last Day in the Field," "Her Quaint Honor," and "Brilliant Leaves." These five, along with other stories not as well known to the general reader, have given Caroline Gordon a reputation, at least among critics, as one of our best short-story writers.[2]

I *"Old Red" and "The Captive"*

The best known and perhaps the best of Caroline Gordon's short stories is "Old Red," a story about Aleck Maury, who is also the protagonist of Miss Gordon's second novel, *Aleck Maury, Sportsman.* Despite the fact that the novel and story include some of the same characters and show us much the same things about Aleck Maury, they are very different in tone and technique. The novel is, of course, more leisurely, more detached, more indirect; and the short story is more intense, more tightly structured. The novel depends for its effects upon the piling up of incidents and details; the short story upon dramatic structure and symbol. The novel is told in the first person by Maury; the short story, from the point of view of the central intelligence, that is, through Aleck Maury's eyes. In the novel we are never very close to the essential Maury, for the first-person point of view as used there is a way of keeping the reader at a distance. In "Old Red," because we see the world through Maury's eyes, we come to share his view of the world. Indeed, Miss Gordon has structured her story in such a way that we actively participate in the discoveries Maury makes about himself and about his world.

"Old Red" is also a subtle story that brief analysis cannot do justice to. It begins quite simply and matter-of-factly with Aleck Maury arriving for a visit at his mother-in-law's house—and then gradually reveals Maury's passion for fishing; his half-comic, half-serious battles with his wife over his addiction to sport; and finally his realization that he Aleck Maury, not the world, is queer. In structure and technique, we are reminded of Henry James's "The Beast in the Jungle" and James Joyce's "The Dead," but Aleck Maury is a hero very different from either John Marcher or Gabriel Conroy. Maury withdraws from the world in order to live, not in order to avoid human involvement. Thus, though the story is ironic, the ironies support rather than undercut Maury's sensibility. One of the chief ironies is that Maury has voluntarily given up his sport (temporarily, of course) in order to visit what is left of his family: his daughter Sarah and her husband Steve and his dead wife's mother-in-law. While in the midst of his family and off his guard, so to speak, he is attacked and his whole existence is called into question. The old war that has been carried on by his wife is resumed by his daughter, Sarah, who is outraged that her father will not give up one afternoon of fishing to attend the funeral of a cousin, the oldest lady in the whole family. Looking around the table as Sarah delivers her lecture on his outrageous behavior Maury catches "the same look in every eye. . . . That look! Sooner or later you met it in every human eye. The thing was to be up and ready, ready to run for your life at a moment's notice. Yes, it had always been like that. It always would be. His fear of them was shot through suddenly with contempt . . ."[3] Before Maury falls asleep that night, he is already planning his escape the next morning to Elk River, one of his favorite fishing haunts.

"The Captive," Caroline Gordon's second most popular short story, is in a more traditional form. It is the first-person account of a pioneer woman taken captive by Indians who undergoes terrible hardships and finally escapes her captors. During her ordeal, she sees her children scalped and her baby dashed against a tree;

and she is carried off to a remote Indian camp where she is forced
to cook for a band of braves and then sold for thirty silver brooches
to the Indian who had murdered her children. The woman, Jinny
Wiley, manages to escape and make her way to a white settlement
in a stockade. She is pursued by the Indians to the bank of the
river where, with the assistance of an old man who is the sole
inhabitant of the stockade, she hastily assembles a raft. Jinny
crosses the river, still pursued by the Indians, and gains the safety
of the stockade. " 'Lord God,' " she cries, looking up at the high
stockade fence all around her, " 'I was lucky to git away from them
Indians.' "

It is interesting that the story of "The Captive" was taken from
an actual account of a pioneer woman.[4] "It was an easy story to
write," Miss Gordon said; "all the details were there. What I did
was to get rid of the Victorian style."[5] In getting rid of the old-
fashioned style with its stilted constructions and abstract language,
Miss Gordon turned a rather flat narrative into a story of personal
heroism. During the course of her flight from the Indians, Jinny
Wiley assumes the proportions of a mythical hero. It is only after
she reaches the safety of the stockade that she reverts to her normal
self. Heroes are made, not born.

Superficially read, the themes of "Old Red" and "The Captive"
are contradictory. "Old Red" appears to deal with freedom from
the strictures of society. "The Captive" pits the safety and security
of the settlement against the dangers and insecurities of life among
the Indians. When Jinny kneels down in the stockade it is not
only for the protection of the walls that she gives thanks, but also
for the moral law and the order those walls represent. Inside is
peace; outside, chaos. "Old Red" deals with the same oppositions,
but from a different vantage point. Maury also struggles with an
"enemy" and he escapes "captivity," not in order to "find himself"
as a Romantic hero might, but to live a life that, whatever its
private pleasures, is disciplined and severely controlled.

II   *Other Aleck Maury Stories*

There are four other stories in *The Forest of the South* in which
Aleck Maury figures: "The Burning Eyes," "To Thy Chamber
Window, Sweet," "One More Time," and "The Last Day in the
Field." The earliest of these, "The Burning Eyes" (which is also
the first chapter of *Aleck Maury, Sportsman*), deals with Maury's
lonely childhood and with the growth of his love of sport. In "To

Thy Chamber Window, Sweet," Maury is forced to choose between courting a pretty widow and going fishing. What makes the choice difficult is that his fishing partner is to be Jim Yost, a genius who "bridged the gap between bait-fishing and fly-casting."[6] There is never really much doubt about which interest will win, for Maury has little taste for the genteel life the widow lives.

"One More Time" and "The Last Day in the Field" treat Aleck Maury more seriously, for in these stories the choice is between living a meaningful life or simply staying alive. "The Last Day in the Field" is perhaps the subtler of the two; indeed, though not as complex, it is in its way as well done as "Old Red." The time of "Last Day in the Field" is November. It has been a long summer, and Aleck Maury is impatiently waiting for cold weather and the beginning of the hunting season. His wife Molly, always the voice of common sense, says, " 'You aren't going to hunt this year, Aleck? Remember how you stayed awake nights last fall with that pain in your leg.' "[7] Maury does not reply. But, as he watches the progress of the light frost—"it creeps higher and higher out of the ground each night of fall," he thinks to himself—"Ha ha. It'll get you yet." When the chilling frost comes and the weather turns cold, Maury is ready for the hunt. He rises early so that Molly will not hear him; wakes Joe Thomas, the boy next door who has two of the best hunting dogs Maury has ever seen; and they drive off together to hunt quail.

It turns out to be a perfect day for hunting; and the country, which is "rough, broken ground, scrub oak with a few gum trees and lots of buckberry bushes," provides all the quail Maury and Joe Thomas can hunt.[8] The dogs, particularly the male, do their work beautifully, and Maury is reminded of a dog he had when he was a young man. Joe Thomas is impatient to shoot and has not learned, as Maury has, the pleasure and wisdom of taking his time and of getting his bird with one, well-placed shot. As Maury silently criticizes Joe Thomas, he also thinks, "It's a wonderful thing to be twenty years old."[9] Maury is in his seventies, a heavy man with a bad leg; and, as the hunt stretches out into the late afternoon and evening, he begins to suffer and sweat. He never complains, of course; and, though he thinks about knocking off at sundown, he cannot since he is one of those men "who lived only for hunting and could never get enough no matter how long the day was."[10] Actually, these words are used by Maury to describe another man who shot himself when he found that his hunting days were over.

Fear of invalidism, of the loss of delight, is something that Maury confronts on a number of occasions; but in this story the positive emotion—the joy of being alive, the pleasure of the hunt—predominates. As the sun goes down and twilight comes, the two hunters are about to call it a day when the dogs pin down a single bird. " 'Your shot,' " Maury says to Joe Thomas; but Joe shakes his head and answers. " 'No, you take it.' "

I went back and flushed the bird. It went skimming along the buckberry bushes that covered that side of the swale. In the fading light I could hardly make it out and I shot too quick. It swerved over the thicket and I let go with the second barrel. It staggered, then zoomed up. Up, up, up, over the rim of the hill and above the tallest hickories. I saw it there for a second, its wings black against the gold light, before, wings still spread, it came whirling down, like an autumn leaf, like the leaves that were everywhere about us, all over the ground.[11]

The conclusion of this story, unpretentious and beautifully evocative, catches exactly in its rhythms and in the image of the hunter, the falling bird, and the autumn leaves not only this last poignant pleasure that Maury gets from hunting but also the immemorial value of his kind of life.

In "One More Time" Aleck Maury is again the narrator, but he is not the central character. He provides sympathetic intelligence by means of which the main character, Bob Reynolds, is presented. As the story opens, Maury is arriving at a boardinghouse on the Elk River. Although we are not told so explicitly, we gather that Maury is in the habit of going there every year and that this is one of his favorite fishing spots. We also learn that he had not planned to go this year but has changed his mind suddenly. During a conversation at supper, Maury is delighted to learn that his old friend Bob Reynolds is also at the hotel, but he is then dismayed to hear that Reynolds' wife is with him. His encounter with Bob Reynolds is even more disquieting. Reynolds is ill, and his wife has come along to make certain he doesn't overexert himself.

The seriousness of Reynolds' illness comes out in a conversation Maury has with the cook, Aunt Zilphy. She says " 'Doctor says it is his liver. He ain't got but a piece of liver. Some little something been eatin' on it. Done et all of it but one little piece and when that's gone he'll be dead.' "[12] Though Maury dismisses Aunt Zilphy as a "morbid old crow," he ponders Reynolds' fate and wonders what he himself would do if he had only six months to live—

"stay very quiet so you might live longer or . . . try to have as good a time as you could?"[13] Since Maury is in good health, it does not occur to him that Reynolds has another choice: suicide. On the pretext of going fishing by himself, Reynolds rows out into the deepest part of "the blue hole" and drowns himself. After his body is found, Reynolds' wife recalls that "he had a queer look on his face when they first started talking about the trip—when he said he wanted to see the old place one more time."[14]

The link between "One More Time" and "The Last Day in the Field" is clear enough. The first mentioned story makes in a negative way rather the same point: Bob Reynolds is one of those rare individuals who enjoys life so passionately that a life of inaction and invalidism is intolerable to him. Simply being alive is not enough. If he cannot fish, if he cannot enjoy life, he will have none of it. This point is brought out early in the story when Aleck Maury contemplates a calendar picture in his room. There is an "eye staring straight ahead, and under it a hand holding a bunch of pencils"—an enigmatic but, as the story develops, a clearly suggestive image of the kind of life Maury and Reynolds both reject— a life of retirement and careful invalidism.[15]

For readers like the O. Henry judge who called Aleck Maury an "old good-for-nothing," Bob Reynolds will perhaps seem little better than a cowardly old man.[16] But as Miss Gordon hints, through Aunt Zilphy's dark mutterings about Reynolds' liver's being devoured, there is something almost Promethean in Reynolds' suffering and courage.

III *Other Heroes*

The protagonist of "Tom Rivers," like Rion Outlaw, Dragging Canoe, General Forrest and Rives Allard, is "fearless, utterly fearless." And like these and other of Miss Gordon's heroes, Tom Rivers cannot stop long in any one place because his fearlessness makes him an outlaw. He left Kentucky because he could not make himself over into the tame, sober person his fiancée wanted him to be. In Texas, Tom Rivers, who was only twenty-three, was generally feared and respected. He was not a quarrelsome man, however; in fact, he was slow to enter a fight, but "when he did go into action, he had a peculiar short, excited laugh."[17] He tossed a man who had attacked him with a pitchfork over a watering trough, took a loaded gun from a gambler and returned it to him butt first, and drove off almost single-handed a thirty-man troop of "Night

Riders." The only way Rivers could be defeated was by being "framed." A man borrowed his gun and shot someone, and Rivers' cousin was deputized to arrest him. Rivers simply rode out of town and was never seen again.

Though technically different, "Her Quaint Honor" and "Mr. Powers" are thematically similar. "Her Quaint Honor" is told in the first person by an insensitive narrator who is so preoccupied by the money he hopes to make from his tobacco crop that he is incapable of appreciating the moral character of his Negro tenant, Tom Doty. "The first year I was at Taylor's Grove," the narrator begins, "I raised ten thousand pounds of tobacco. Five thousand pounds of lugs and seconds and five thousand pounds of prime leaf. And, boy, was it prime! I ought to have got thirty cents for that leaf, the way it was selling that year. But I didn't get but fifteen. That yellow wife of Tom Doty's was the cause of that."[18] Then he proceeds to tell a tale that reveals the drunkenness and sensuality of a white man who attempts to seduce Tom Doty's wife, Tom Doty's fury, and the narrator's "heroic" sacrifice of his tobacco crop in order to keep Tom Doty from cutting the white man, Bud Asbury, with a razor. What the perceptive reader sees, of course, is that the narrator is a man with few interests outside of making money, that the only "fault" Tom Doty's wife has is being too much alive and that Tom Doty is a hero, a man with a deeply ingrained sense of honor. For, even though his color puts him in a position inferior to Bud Asbury, he is ready to fight to save his wife's honor.[19]

"Mr. Powers" is told from the point of view of a city couple, Jack and Ellen Crombie, who have moved to the country. They "take on" a white tenant named Mr. Powers and later discover that he is an accused murderer and is to be tried for killing his six-year-old son with an ax. Mr. Powers had come home unexpectedly and found his wife in the embrace of the hired hand; and, in a moment of blind anger he had taken his ax and unintentionally struck his son. The country woman who brings the story to the Crombies is outraged by this "murder," but Miss Gordon shows that Mr. Powers' crime, paradoxically, is the product of his virtue; for he has acted only because he loves his wife and because he has, like Tom Doty, the simple man's deeply ingrained sense of honor.

In "Her Quaint Honor," Miss Gordon employs irony to make her point. In "Mr. Powers," she uses perceptive city people to arrive at the truth about Mr. Powers. Mrs. Crombie is determined to ask Mr. Powers about some trees he has promised to cut for them (as payment for trees he has taken out of their woods), but at the end of the story, when she sees Mr. Powers in his wagon coming down the road, his head bare and his face turned toward a spectacular view of the river and valley that she herself has been admiring, she refuses to ask for payment.

IV   *"All the Lovers Love the Spring"*

"All the Lovers Love the Spring" is a quiet horror story told by a forty-two-year-old spinster who is very proud of the fact that she is a Fuqua, a family that has been prominent in and around Fuqua, Kentucky, for generations. Her "third cousin, Roger Treadwell, is president of the First National Bank . . . president of the Chamber of Commerce and permanent treasurer of the Community Chest and chairman of the board of directors of the hospital."[20] Miss Fuqua is even more impressed with her own family and her own childhood which she unintentionally reveals to have been passive and dull. When she was sixteen, she went to Bardstown Academy; and her cousin Roger went to Webb. The first night Roger came home from Webb, he asked her for a date to go to a dance. Miss Fuqua tells exactly what she wore and what food she and Roger consumed after the party. She also remembers that she knew she should not go inside a place "like Shorty Raymond's" so that she and Roger ate their "sandwiches, Coke, and orangeade" outside.

The final revelation about Miss Fuqua comes at the end of the story when she announces that she has taken up the hobby of hunting and eating mushrooms. The hobby gives her an excuse to get away from her invalid mother who, we finally learn, has dominated her all of her life. Out in the woods under a blossoming pear tree the "petals looked like sea shells. I stood under the tree and watched all those festoons of little shells floating up over my head, up, up, up into the bluest sky I've ever seen and wished that I didn't have to go home. Mama's room always smells of camphor. You notice it after you've been out in the fresh air."

V   *Civil War Stories*

There are three stories in *Forest of the South* about the Civil War—the title story, "Hear the Nightingale Sing," and "Ice House." "Forest of the South" is about a Northern officer who falls in love with a Southern girl on whose plantation he is quartered. At the end of the story, the girl surrenders her cousin to her Yankee lover; the cousin, who is in federal uniform, is doomed to be shot as a spy. The story ends with a startling, but in retrospect, well-prepared-for reversal. The Southern officer reveals that his cousin is mad. In assuming responsibility for her, the Northern officer has given his prisoner a strange victory.

"Hear the Nightingale Sing" is an untraditional handling of a traditional Civil War situation: a Yankee soldier tries to take a pet mule away from a high-spirited, young Southern woman. Instead of killing the soldier, which is what the traditional "belle" would do under the circumstances, Miss Gordon's heroine only dreams of doing so. She does struggle with the soldier over possession of her mule, but she is easily thrust aside, and the soldier rides away. Miss Gordon's heroine does triumph, however. The mule throws the soldier and tramples him to death. This ending also comes as a shock; but, again, the shock has been well prepared for.

The best of these three Civil War stories is "The Ice House," which deserves to be better known. It is written in a spare, terse style somewhat reminiscent of Hemingway's early stories that Miss Gordon may have learned from him; the matter and the manner, however, are her own. The time of "Ice House" is two years after the end of the Civil War. The place is somewhere in the South in and around an old ice house where the bodies of Union soldiers were hastily buried during a battle in 1862. The characters are two Southern boys—Doug, age sixteen; Raeburn, age fifteen—and a Yankee contractor, whose name is never mentioned. The boys have been hired by the contractor to go into the ice house to dig out the skeletons of the Union soldiers while he remains outside to arrange the bones in the pine coffins which he will later deliver to the United States government at so much "a head." The boys arrive on the job early, work all day hacking out skeletons, and are told by the contractor at the end of the day that their services will not be required again.

The older boy, Doug, is surprised; for the contractor had said that there would be another day's work. But the boys take their pay and prepare to leave. Doug, however, hangs back to see what the contractor is going to do. He watches for a few moments and then calls Raeburn to him, and together they spy through the bushes at the contractor standing before the semicircle of pine coffins scratching his bald head. Suddenly he stoops and begins to distribute the bones in the coffins that are still empty. "What you reckon he's doing, Doug?" Raeburn asks. "He's dividing up them skeletons so he can git paid double,"Doug says.[21] The boys get up and slip off silently through the underbrush. When they come to a fork in the path Doug stops. "There ain't a whole man in ary one of them boxes," he says; and he slaps his leg and rocks in laughter, "If that ain't a Yankee fer ye!"[22]

It is not too surprising that a reviewer for the *Saturday Review of Literature* took offense at this story and called it "little more than a Southern jibe at Yankee slickness," but it is surprising that Andrew Lytle, who approves of the story, reads it in much the same way.[23] "The Yankee contractor," he writes,

> is a symbol of the revolutionary change in American society, the acceptance of materialism as the final value in the state. It is this which has triumphed in the Civil War. The defeat of the Confederacy destroyed in the Union the restraints of the checks and balances which took into account the depravity of man, at the same time as socially the values of a traditional hierarchy of relationships were smashed. Death, of course, is the final comment on matter. It reduces it to dust and the bare bone. By implication life conceived only in terms of the material aims makes of it a living death, by denying the spirit. The contractor is the embodiment of this denial in his own person and as representative of the Yankee attitude.[24]

To read "Ice House" in purely regional terms, however, is to misread it. Miss Gordon is not so naïve as to believe that acquisitiveness is the exclusive property of Yankees. Indeed, her story suggests something very different, as a careful reading shows.

"Ice House" begins with Doug "waiting where the paths forked as Raeburn came through the woods." This first sentence hints at what is to be an important difference between the two boys. Doug is a "go-getter"; Raeburn, as we gradually learn, takes life more leisurely. Doug's first remark is to chastise his friend for his lateness. "I thought you wasn't coming," Doug said. "I thought you'd just about give it out and decided you wasn't coming." Raeburn's response indicates that he puts other things above money-grubbing: "I had to get my breakfast. I ain't going to work for nobody on an empty stomach . . . . Tain't more'n six o'clock anyhow."[25] At heart, Doug is a Ben Franklin moralist. "Well," he says, "the way I look at it is if you going to work for a man you ought to work for him." Up to this point, even experienced readers may be unsure about whose side the author is on in the moral tug-of-war. And it is an important part of her strategy to remain hidden, allowing the reader to respond for himself. There is always the risk, of course, that the reader will make the wrong response.

A writer like John Steinbeck, for example, would not take such a risk; he would make certain that the characters were properly tagged. Miss Gordon does take the risk, for her strategy is to direct the reader's response through art rather than through sentiment. When she shifts point of view to Raeburn, we see him watching his "skinny shadow racing with him, over the new green shoots of pokeberry and sassafras," and we learn that "it occurred to him that it was the middle of April. The dogwoods were all in full flower. Channel cat ought to be biting."[26] This passage it the first clear signal of the author's attitude, but still it is one that requires an unconventional response. Anyone familiar with the Aleck Maury stories knows, of course, that Miss Gordon sympathizes with Raeburn's longing to go fishing; but the sympathy is not forced on the reader. The superiority of Raeburn's longing is presented through contrast to the work that Doug is willing, even anxious, to do; dig skeletons out of the frozen ground. Indeed, it it from Raeburn's point of view that what the Yankee contractor and Doug stand for is, finally, to be judged.

When Doug says, a paragraph or so later, "Handlin' a dead Yankee ain't no more to *me* than handlin' a dead hawg," his declaration does not derive from the author's regional prejudices.[27] Rather, it is her attempt to characterize Doug. Furthermore, the actions of the Yankee contractor are not simply the author's way of jibing at "Yankee slickness"; they indicate that the contractor, like Doug, exhibits morally repellent values. The contractor is superficially affable, and, like Doug, an early riser who talks the language of the go-getter: "Now what we got to do is fill the boxes up. The sooner we get them boxes filled up the sooner we get done and the sooner we get done the sooner you get your money . . . . Ain't that right, Bud?"[28]

With the same care and restraint with which she has introduced the three main characters, Miss Gordon proceeds to describe the grisly contents of the ice house. Her description of the dead soldiers, though unsparingly realistic, reveals an attitude very different from Doug's or the contractor's: "The skeletons were level with the earth. There was a man's skull on top of the pile. The eye sockets turned toward the door, the ribs and long leg bones slanting away diagonally across the heap, as if the man had flung himself down face forward to look out over the field. Where the light from the open door fell the bones were pale, almost white, but the bones that showed here and there underneath were darker. There was moss on some of them."[29] The description of the skeleton lying "as if the man had flung himself down" makes us suddenly aware of the humanity of those who died, not as an enemy soldier to be despised, but as a man who lived once and who even while dying had turned himself in order to "look out over the field" where the fighting had been and perhaps was still going on.

This apparently objective description has actually pointed us toward the major contrast in the story, that between those who have made a personal commitment to a cause and those who, like the contractor, merely profit from it. After the author has made us feel the humanity of the dead soldiers, she proceeds to describe the corruption that has taken place and the calloused attitude of the living whose only concern for the dead is the profit that is to be made from them.

After the boys enter the ice house, a kind of opposition between them and the contractor develops. This conflict is natural; he is an outsider, and they are friends. But the significant opposition is not, as Andrew Lytle apparently believes, between the Yankee as the embodiment of unchecked materialism and the boys as innocent and sensitive to the physical nausea of death whose "feeling and reflections are all for life."[30] A close look at the dramatic structure of the story shows that, on the contrary, Miss Gordon continues to maintain the differences she has already established between Doug and Raeburn and that, as the story nears its close, these differences take on more sinister implications. These differences are also even more indirectly indicated. Doug does the work quickly and efficiently. When Raeburn volunteers to get down into the slimy pit to hack out the skeletons, Doug insists that he stay on. "It'd just be wasting time now if we change places."[31] During the lunch period, Raeburn is so nauseated he cannot eat his lunch; Doug has no such difficulty. And Doug's concern with the skeletons is all business: how he is paid, by the day or so much for the job? Raeburn, on the contrary, talks about fishing and tells the Yankee contractor the best way to catch a channel cat.

That Doug is as practical as the Yankee contractor is further shown by his failure to sense the probable feelings of Mrs. Porter, a neighbor woman to whom the Yankee goes to borrow a ladder. Raeburn senses immediately how Mrs. Porter will feel. "Do you reckon they'll lend him a ladder?" Raeburn asks. "Shore they will," Doug says; "'Tain't nothin' to lend anybody a ladder."[32] When Raeburn reminds Doug that Mrs. Porter had three sons killed in the War by Yankees, Doug laughs: "This feller never killed no Confederates."[33] We see in this exchange between Raeburn and Doug a corruption deeper than the Yankee contractor's. The contractor is merely an outsider; but Doug, a Southerner, ought to at least sense how Mrs. Porter will feel. His final remarks on the Yankee's shrewdness—dividing up the skeletons to get paid double—is not just a jibe at Yankee slickness; it is a comment on Doug himself and, by extension, on the qualities that he embodies. The final scene, in which Dougs slaps his thigh and rocks with laughter in high appreciation of Yankee cunning, bears comparison to the conclusion of *The Hamlet* by William Faulkner, a novel on somewhat the same theme.

Another story likely to be misread is "The Enemies," an early story on one of Miss Gordon's major themes, personal honor. "The Enemies" begins with the sheriff "meeting two dark figures at the head of the stairs." "Step, up, boy," the sheriff says. And "the Negro manacled at wrist and ankle took his place on the iron trap." The sheriff says, "Anything to say, boy?" And the condemned man replies in a "throaty voice," "I ain't got nothing to say, Boss."[34] The trap is sprung, and the body falls with a thud to the floor below. The reaction of the two white newspaper reporters is depicted. They are blasé. One of them lights a cigarette before answering the question of a young Negro, "Is he dead, Boss?" The reporter for the *Press-Scimitar* replies, "As a door nail or will be in another minute."

The scene then shifts to a café where three people are gathered —a grizzled old Negro man, an old woman fanning the fire, and a gigantic young Negro man whose eyes are red-rimmed. The boy, Eugene, appears with the news of the death; and our first impression is that the family of the man who has been executed is waiting in numbed anguish for news of his death. We learn, however, that these are the dead man's enemies. The old woman is the mother of a young woman he had murdered; the old man, the father; and the gigantic younger man, the husband. The old woman, Aunt Perea, wants to know if he repented before he died. When Eugene says that he did not, she is driven nearly out of her mind. The husband of the murdered woman sits brooding in a rocking chair, his coon dog at his feet. He alternates between spasms of grief over his dead wife and boasts about his physical prowess: "Thirty-four years old, sound as a nut. Ain't no man on Big Bend can put me on my back. Ain't no man anywhere on the river . . . ."[35]

The narrator then focuses on the boy who is being urged to eat by the old man, Uncle Lias. The boy puts a morsel of food

in his mouth but then lets it fall. Uncle Lias looks around at the dog
lying flat on the floor,

paws limp, head thrown back at an unnaturally sharp angle. As Uncle
Lias watched the thin line of red at his throat widened and suddenly
spilled over into blood.

Uncle Lias took a step forward. "Put that razor down, Gunter!"

The big Negro was straightening up to his full height. His rapt
eyes gazed over their heads. One hand was thrust out as if to ward
off approach. The other wove bright circles in the smoky air.

"Coming!" he shouted. "Coming. I gives you your time and you
didn't get here. Now I'm coming.'"

The circling hand drew in, hovered a moment. Then the razor
dropped to the floor as the man staggered and fell face forward across
the table.

Uncle Lias shrank back into the chimney corner. A woman's shrill
cry rose:

"*Done gone to meet him!* Oh, my baby. She can res' easy now!"[36]

On the face of it, this is a rather familiar story, like Faulkner's "That Evening Sun," about terror and violence among primitive Negroes. But it is not told simply for the shock and horror. It
is a story about honor and revenge. To the white reporter, the
murderer is "dead as a doornail", but to Gunter, husband of the
murdered woman, he is still "out there," still to be dealt with. The
slaughtered dog, the suicide, and the fanatical cry of the old
woman are not meant to display the primitive emotions of the
characters but to suggest the passionate depths of their feelings.

VI *"Brilliant Leaves" and "Summer Dust"*

Two stories that do not quite seem to belong with the rest of
those in *The Forest of the South* are "Brilliant Leaves" and "Summer Dust." "Brilliant Leaves" is a beautifully constructed minor
tragedy in which a boy and a girl who have been separated for
the summer are reunited in the woods at a summer resort where
their families have cabins. The boy has been working in town,
and the girl has remained at the resort with her family. As the
boy walks through the woods to meet his girl, the ground is covered with brilliant red leaves of fall. The couple finds a little out-
of-the-way spot in the woods where the trees have kept their leaves
and the grass is still green. After an interlude in which their love
is rekindled they go for a hike and come upon a waterfall, Bridal
Falls, where the girl wants to climb up the steep rock, and the boy

reluctantly consents. The climb is high and the rocks slippery because of the water.

As the girl steps from one rock to another, she slips and falls backward onto the rocks below. The boy clambers down and finds her, moaning, her eyes open. "I've got to get some help," the boy says, and goes racing off through the dead leaves toward the cluster of summer houses "that no matter how fast he ran kept always just ahead of him" and seemed in danger of sliding "off the hill and leave him running forever through these woods, over these dead leaves."[37] Andrew Lytle has suggested that "Brilliant Leaves" is about the boy's failure to live up to his responsibilities as a man: in permitting the girl to have her way, he indirectly contributes to her death.[38] But his interpretation seems too moralistic a reading; moreover, the boy is too young to assume such responsibilities. Because he loves the girl and does what she wants to do, "Brilliant Leaves," it would seem, is about the tragedy of death that comes in the midst of life. Its final impact is somewhat like that of *Romeo and Juliet* or, to select a more recent example, *A Farewell to Arms*.

"Summer Dust" is a different kind of story from the rest of those collected in *Forest of the South*. There is the same enigmatic quality, the understatement, the restraint, and the feeling that a great deal more is being implied than is actually said; but, where Miss Gordon's stories are usually dramatic and more or less "objective" accounts of heroes seen at a distance, the point of view in "Summer Dust" is more closely identified with the protagonist, Sally Ellis, a young girl living in the country somewhere in Tennessee or Kentucky; and the point of the story is deeply involved in Sally's emotional responses. Miss Gordon's technique for rendering this emotion is to give us, one after the other, four incidents unconnected in time and place. We do not see the logic of these connections, but we are made to feel them through the tone, the rhythm of the sentences, and certain key phrases and images.

In Part I of the story, Sally is on her way to pick peaches with an old Negro servant and her grandchildren. Sally is very much aware that she is not one of them; and, as she walks along the dusty road, she says to herself, "I am not a nigger. I'm the only one who's not a nigger." The peach trees happen to be in the yard of a house rented from Sally's family, and the white woman who lives there is enraged when Sally and the Negroes come to get "her" peaches. " Naw, they ain't youah peaches," Aunt Maria says.

"They's Miss Molly and Mistuh Ed's peaches."³⁹ When the woman calls that "Miss Molly Murray and Mistuh Ed Murray is low-down dawgs," Aunt Maria, smiling, replies, "They may be dawgs, but they laks peaches. Come on, chillun, pick 'em up." Sally, how-ever, "didn't pick up any peaches. She didn't want any peaches."

In Part I, Sally has had an introduction to human meanness and suffering; and, repelled by them, she longs for a better world. This yearning is brought out dramatically in the incident of the peach-es, but it is also underscored earlier in this section when Son, a Negro boy, runs ahead, making the trail of a great snake in the dust. Sally thinks of the snakes that her brother and the old cook Marie always kill and hang on the fence and of the yellow place they make so that "you couldn't climb there." Her mind then re-calls some words of a fairy tale: " 'But what will I eat?' asked the little Princess. 'Roots and berries; do not be afraid, my child,' said the fairy godmother."⁴⁰

In Part II, Sally is in the dark woods on her black horse; and she is carried to a place where she thinks nobody had been for a long time. But she finds the moss crushed and what appears to be half of a golden earring. Immediately her imagination trans-forms that object into a gypsy woman going through woods. In Part III, Sally and her brothers, Tom and Alec, are driving to Ellengowan to visit their grandparents. On the way, they talk about going to see Aunt Silvy; and, when Sally asserts that she is not going to see the old Negro woman, Tom says, "You better. She'll put something on you."⁴¹ Tom tells Sally that Aunt Silvy is a hundred and fifty years old and that she likes to drink blood: "That's what makes her so strong."⁴² But Sally is forced to go to see "mammy," a ritual that all visitors are obliged to perform. Sally walks to the cabin alone and reluctantly steps over the thresh-old into the dark cabin. At first it is so dark she can see nothing, and she stands still until a voice calls out, "Who dat?" When she replies, "It's Sally Ellis," the voice says, "Whyn't you come heah and shake hands with me? Wheah youah mannahs?"⁴³ Sally takes the old woman's hand and remembers the awful stories she has heard about her and thinks that her strangely sick smell is the odor of the blood she has eaten. Finally, Aunt Silvy's daughter calls her away; "You bettuh run 'long to the house. Them boys'll eat up all that ice cream."⁴⁴ Sally runs as fast as she can to the house, not out of hunger but out of very fear.

Part IV deals with another experience but nevertheless draws together the images and themes of the three earlier sections. When

Sally Ellis is walking down a country road with her brother Tom, who is now sixteen, they meet an older cousin Robert; and the two boys begin to talk about a country trial that Robert has been recently involved in. From their conversation, it appears that Robert and another boy have been intimate with a girl named Ada Peters; and the trial was being conducted in order to determine the father of her baby. The other boy, Virgil Stokes, had admitted "it was him all right":

> And then the judge asked him if he didn't know it was a very serious thing to violate the age of consent, and he said he didn't know there was such thing.
> Tom laughed until you could hear the echo in the wood.
> "I'll bet he'll know what the age of consent is next time," [he said.]
> "I bet he will," Robert said.
> Tom threw back his head and laughed again.
> "Yeah," he said. "He'll know what it is next time."[45]

In the conclusion of this story, the imagination of Sally rejects the sordid world evoked by the conversation of the two boys; and she conjures up in the language of the fairy tale a place superior to this predatory world in which appetites are supreme. In "Summer Dust" Miss Gordon simply juxtaposes these two worlds—the natural one devoid of any redeeming vision and the fairy-tale one evoked by the protagonist's reading. Many years later, after her religious conversion, Miss Gordon rewrote this story, gave it the title of "One Against Thebes," a mythological underpinning, and sharper religious implication.[46]

What is especially interesting about "Summer Dust," Miss Gordon's first published short story, is that it reflects with uncanny accuracy the direction her own personal life was to take, as well as the future development of her fiction. Sally Ellis, like Lucy Lewis of *Strange Children* and Vera Claiborne of *The Malefactors,* unconsciously rejects the brutality and ugliness of this world in favor of the enchanted world of the imagination. The artistic implications are clear enough, but the religious and mystical implications become clearer only when seen from the vantage point of Miss Gordon's "Catholic" fiction. What Sally Ellis really longs for is a transcending religious experience.

VII *Old Red and Other Stories*

In 1963 Caroline Gordon published her second volume of short stories, *Old Red and Other Stories.* Of the nine pieces in this book, three were new, one was an old story rewritten and retitled, and the remaining five had appeared in her first collection *The Forest of the South* (1945). Among the new stories, "Emmanuele! Emmanuele!" is the longest and most controversial. It is based on an anecdote Miss Gordon heard about André Gide, but the implications of this story go farther and deeper than fictionalized biography.[47] The protagonist of "Emmanuele! Emmanuele!" is a French man of letters named Gillaume Fäy, who is seen through the eyes of a young American poet and college professor Robert Heyward. Heyward, who greatly admires Fäy, becomes through influential friends the great man's secretary for a short time. During a visit in North Africa with Fäy, Heywood hears disparaging criticism of Fäy from a cousin, a friend, and a colleague of Fäy's. The cousin finds Fäy's practice of writing while seated before a mirror a form of perversion and maintains that Fäy's marriage has never been consummated. The literary colleague contends that Fäy's influence on contemporary letters has been poisonous. Heywood, however, cannot square these criticisms with his own sympathetic response to Fäy and his writing.

Only after Heywood visits Fäy's home in Normandy and meets Fäy's wife does he begin to discover the truth. Fäy's wife is, properly, an old woman; for she has spent herself laboring. Fäy is youthful-seeming because he has never given himself to anything but self-love. After a short stay in the house of his patron, Heywood senses that these two people do not react to each other or do not seem to live in the same world; but he still does not understand the meaning of their separation. A conflict between Fäy and Emmanuele, as Fäy calls his wife, reveals the significant difference between them. While Fäy is working on a long poem about Hercules, and Heywood is typing it, Fäy needs a phrase or two from some letters that he has ostensibly written to his wife. These letters were mentioned by Fäy in his journal as love letters which are to be published after his death and which are to reveal a side of him never before exposed to the public. The letters are locked in a desk, and the key is possessed by Emmanuele. Instead of giving Heywood the key, as Fäy had requested her to do, she herself goes to Fäy's study; and, when Heywood a little later approaches the study door, he hears whimpering and crying and then Fäy's voice saying, "We can never get them back. . . . *She* burned them." When Heywood left to get the key to the desk, the shutters in Fäy's study were open, the sunlight was pouring in, and Fäy was looking young and jaunty. The shutters are later closed and "Now it was dark. She must have drawn the blinds before she left. The old man's head and shoulders would show hunched against the pale-colored jalousies. Ever afterwards he was to think of that head as hooded, but the eyes, the eyes that gleamed so merry, so mottled! They would be black now—twin prisons in which a creature that had once sported in the sun would sit forever in darkness."[48]

When *Old Red and Other Stories* appeared in 1964, one reviewer complained that "Emmanuele! Emmanuele!" was a pointless story since the details about André Gide on which Gillaume Fäy was based were already well known.[49] Such complaints miss the point. Miss Gordon has used facts about André Gide, not to say something about *him*, but to say something about life itself, something she had been saying in a number of other stories and novels. Gillaume Fäy before his fall was a pagan creature who, his protests to the contrary, never really suffered because he never cared enough for anyone to suffer. The famous love letters, written supposedly to his wife, were really addressed to himself; and the reason Fäy whimpers and cries when he discovers that the letters have been burnt is that, for the first time in his life, he has lost something of value. The description at the close of the story of Fäy sitting hunched and dejected is almost too allegorical a statement about the change that has taken place in him. His youthfulness and his jauntiness— the symbols of his paganism—have given way to marks of age and suffering. By being made to suffer, Fäy has left that demon world —the same underworld inhabited by a number of Miss Gordon's villians—and entered the human world.

VIII   *"The Presence"*

"The Presence" is a new story about Aleck Maury, a Maury who is now seen and judged from the standpoint of Christian faith. In this story Maury is old and has had to give up sport entirely, but he has taken refuge in a boarding house run by a couple who stand between Maury and a death-in-life emptiness. Maury is very fond of his landlady, Jenny Mowbray, a plump, good-natured woman who runs her kitchen with skill and enthusiasm and who takes a personal interest in the lives of her boarders. As the story opens, Maury is verbally crossing swords on the veranda with another boarder, a pale, washed-out spinster who sustains herself with health foods and transcendentalism. Their conflict is interrupted by the arrival of Jenny's husband, Jim, a handsome sunburned man who shares Maury's enthusiasm for sport. Jim Mowbray, who has been hunting, is very pleased with the performance of his setter. Through Jim, Maury relives his hunting days. He takes over the feeding of the dog and almost feels in the process that it is he "making his way home, at day's end, by the slanting rays of the sun, his game bag heavy on his shoulder...."[50]

Maury is happy living with the Mowbrays. He still eats with his old relish and enjoys making innocently flirtatious conversation with a pretty but too-thin blond divorcée named Riva Gaines. That night at supper, Maury also admires Jenny Mowbray who has just returned from a visit to her sick father. But talk of illness chills Maury, particularly Jenny's remark about her father losing his faculties: "A terrible thing to lose your faculties. . . . What a terrible thing it would be if he lost his mind that to him such a kingdom was!"[51] Maury is cheered by Jenny's maternal interest in him. She has had Dr. Weathers write a prescription out for him; and, by the time Jim Mowbray comes to the supper table, Maury has forgotten about his physical deterioration and is joking with the blond divorcée about marriage. Before the evening is over, Jenny discovers that her husband has been having an affair with Riva Gaines and that he wants to marry her. When Jenny announces to Maury that she is going to sell the boardinghouse and return to Kentucky, Maury is dejected—his pleasant, comfortable world has crashed. That night Maury has another quarrel with Miss Gilbert, and he cries out passionately,"*Women* . . . I've been watching them. They'll rock the world if they don't look out."[52]

It is not women, however, who are at the root of the trouble but the men who have allowed women to take over the world. Maury muses: "There were no women in his life now, and yet he seemed to have been in servitude to them all his life."[53] This conclusion is exaggerated, of course, but it contains a general truth. Instead of dominating their women as they were meant to do, men allow women to dominate them. Jim Mowbray will be divorced and remarried "before he knew what had happened to him." But then Jim "was not a man to stand up to women."[53] Paradoxically, however, women—or at least the right woman—can help save a man's immortal soul. Maury thinks of his Aunt Vic who, when he was orphaned at four, took him to live with her, not to teach him Latin and mathematics as she pretended, but to save his soul. Aunt Vic was a devout Catholic and she made Maury and his cousin Julian kneel and pray at command, the way a bird dog is taught to charge and point. But on her deathbed, beside which the young Maury sat, Aunt Vic saw a presence that he could not see and when she died, he ran out to tell the others, weeping and wondering "What it was he could not see." It is Miss Gilbert, ignorant of the true meaning of her words, who correctly diagnoses the situation. "There's no faith in men."[55] It is faith, Miss Gordon suggests, that Maury has always lacked. For Maury, like Stephen Lewis of *The Strange Children,* is outside the Church, feels his alienation but is not able to cross the chasm of doubt. In a sense, "The Presence" is a rewriting of Aleck Maury's old dilemma, bringing it into line with Miss Gordon's Catholicism. In the earlier stories, Aleck Maury was frequently depressed by the prospect of death, but he always managed to find some way to cheer himself up, usually through sport. In "The Presence," Maury is made to face the issue and is not permitted any earthly consolation. Indeed, he is faced with a meaningful death but is denied the power to unlock the meaning.

IX *"The Petrified Woman*

The third new story in this collection is "The Petrified Woman," which is told in the first person by a narrator looking back on a childhood experience. The narrator does not judge or evaluate; she simply reports what she saw and felt when she was a child. The occasion for this recollection is a family reunion "held at a place called Arthur's cave" one memorable year when Hilda, the narrator's cousin, had a new stepmother, a Cousin Eleanor from Birmingham. What made the reunion memorable for the child was, ostensibly, the beauty of the stepmother who dressed in a long, white gown and wore diamonds in her ears and on her breast in the shape of a cross. But what really made the narrator remember this occasion so vividly, the reader sees, was the suppressed conflict between Cousin Eleanor and her husband Tom.

Cousin Tom drinks too much; and, for a time, there is some doubt about whether Eleanor's coldness to him is the cause or the result of his drinking. Gradually, the reader realizes that Tom's misbehaving is in large part caused by his wife's lack of feeling. This insight is dramatized by an incident involving a "petrified woman" in a traveling carnival that stops near the cave where the reunion is in progress. The narrator and Cousin Hilda go to see the carnival freak who is called Stella, "the petrified woman." Cousin Tom, who accompanies them, is struck by the fact that Stella is beautiful and also petrified. At dinner that night he announces to the assembled guests that he is in love with the petrified woman. When his wife asks for her name, Tom replies, " 'Stell-a. The One and

Only Stell-a!' "[56] The reader, of course, knows that the real petrified woman is Cousin Eleanor.

"The Petrified Woman" deals with a motif encountered before in Miss Gordon's fiction. Cousin Eleanor resembles women like the wife of Nicholas Llewellyn in *Penhally,* Elsie Manigault in *Women on the Porch,* Isabel Reardon of *Strange Children,* and Cynthia Vail of *The Malefactors*—women who hate what is natural and who attempt to dominate their men. The conclusion of the story—in which the narrator remembers exactly how Cousin Eleanor looked in her long white dress, walking over to the window where the water glints on the rocks and "Cousin Tom is still lying there on the floor" with his head cut by a wine glass—nicely catches the point of the story: Eleanor's deadness and Tom's degradation.

X   *"One Against Thebes"*

"One Against Thebes," a rewritten version of Caroline Gordon's first published story, "Summer Dust," is interesting for several reasons. Essentially, "One Against Thebes" is the same story told in "Summer Dust"; but it is reorganized, rather severely cut, and considerably heightened in tone. By judicious reselection of detail, by conversion of a number of highly colloquial and dialect expressions into more formal English, and by the insertion into the body of the story several allusions to classical myth, Miss Gordon has converted a loosely constructed realistic short story into a highly suggestive poetic one.

"One Against Thebes" is about evil, as was "Summer Dust"; but the evil has been given a historical-mythical basis in addition to a Naturalistic one. The reference to Thebes and to Heracles are intended to place a small girl, the protagonist, in a tradition which the author sees as coming in a straight line from Classical times down to our own day. For many readers, the connection between Heracles and a small girl in the twentieth-century rural South may seem farfetched, but Miss Gordon has managed to join these in a convincing relationship. She accomplishes this parallel outside the story through the title "One Against Thebes" and by the epigraph, "That you shall forever hold this city safe from the men of Thebes, the dragon's sons." But the connection is made within the story by the child's father who is learned in Classical literature and who bridges the two worlds by expressing in his idomatic English the truth of the Greek myths and their applicability as paradigms for our own times. The Thebans were said to have descended from dragons and their early ancestors to have serpent's coils. When the child's brother rejects this statement with "I wouldn't want to be made out of no old snake's teeth..." and the father replies: "It's none of your business, Sir, how you are made.... Snaps and snails and puppy dogs' tails I've been told."[57]

Miss Gordon's story suggests that, if modern men do not have serpent's tails, they are nevertheless capable of behaving with serpentine cunning. This suggestion is pointed up early in the story through the description of Son, the Negro boy, who runs from one side of the road to another making a trail like a serpent in the coils of which the child and her other Negro companions are following. Man's capacity for evil is also emphasized by the events of the story itself in which character after character commits some act of cruelty and spite against a fellow mortal. The only redeemed person in the story is the child who is inspired through a fairy-story book to do something generous and who envisions a world better than the one through which she must walk. She gives her fairy-tale book to the Negro boy Son—slips it into his pocket, not wanting to be seen or thanked and knowing that she will never see it again. At the end of the story, as she goes along the road kicking up the summer dust, she deliberately recalls the words of the fairy godmother from one of her fairy tales, describing a fairy-tale paradise.

"One against Thebes" not only is interesting as an effective short story, it is also a useful lesson in the art of fiction when put along side "Summer Dust." More important, is what "One Against Thebes" tells us about Miss Gordon's career: it shows that, though her fiction underwent significant changes after her religious conversion, the religious implication was already present in her first published short story.

CHAPTER 12

Conclusion

*There are ... great writers who
are not read properly in their own
day for the reason, perhaps, that
their readers are not yet born.
What they have to say to their
own generation is said so at cross-
purposes and with such apparent
irrelevance that it is not understood.*

—Caroline Gordon,
How to Read a Novel[1]

A CRITIC who focuses exclusively on the work of one writer
and who lives for a time with the sensibility of that writer
may come to feel that his subject's work is not only unique but self-
generated as well. That risk is one of the hazards, but also one of
the pleasures, of literary criticism. Caroline Gordon's work is
unique in the best sense: it is not imitative; it is clearly a product
of a fully integrated sensibility. But, even a casual comparison of
her fiction with that of the leading writers of her time reveals
similarities and also possible influences.

I   *The Traditional Elements*

In concern for craft and technique, Caroline Gordon has much
in common with James Joyce and Ernest Hemingway. She shares
their concept of fiction as an impersonal art, and she uses natural
objects symbolically as a way of transcending the limitations of
one-dimensional realism. She also employs, particularly in her short

stories, the dramatic method, understatement, and irony. Almost nothing is directly stated, and everything is dramatized. In achieving this dramatic quality, Miss Gordon has gone beyond either Joyce or Hemingway, or one might more accurately say that she has returned to ancient times and has taken as her models the Greek tragedies, particularly the plays of Sophocles. For in their stateliness, their restraint, and their tightly structured actions, Miss Gordon's novels and stories often remind us more of *Oedipus Rex* than of a Hemingway or a Joyce novel.

Miss Gordon's early style, which is terse and restrained—particularly in short stories such as "The Enemies" and "The Ice House"— reminds us of the famous Hemingway style of the 1920's. We do not imply that her early style is imitative—it is more natural than Hemingway's—but only that she may have learned from Hemingway the art of economy, an art that is closely related to the principle of allowing an action to speak for itself. Miss Gordon's later style is more relaxed and supple; it still catches the rhythms of the spoken language; but it is always formal, even correct. The effect of this style is to bring the reader close to the scene and the characters but never to involve him emotionally as does, for example, the style of a writer like William Faulkner.

In Miss Gordon's choice of heroes and in her view that the love of a man for a woman is an essential ingredient of fiction, she has more in common with Hemingway and Scott Fitzgerald than Joyce, though perhaps what is shared is not an influence as much as a common inheritance. Like Hemingway, and to some extent like Fitzgerald, Miss Gordon's interest often focuses on a brave man who faces danger and defeat. Victory, however, is not so much a matter of a physical triumph as in having stood the test. In fact, all three writers share this kind of Jamesian preference for the moral rather than for the physical triumph. A significant difference is in the tone, in the degree of acceptance of the hero's tragic end. Hemingway and Fitzgerald are both more sympathetic, even sentimental (Hemingway in particular) about the suffering of their heroes. For Miss Gordon, defeat and suffering are stoically accepted, we might almost say welcomed, as confirmation that the lot of man is inevitably tragic.

With William Faulkner, Caroline Gordon shares an attachment to the Southern past, one which is not just sentimental unwillingness to accept change but an attachment to the agrarian-rural way of life and a deep aversion to the commercial, rational, and theoretic quality of city culture. Both Faulkner and Miss Gordon feel that there is a value in the land itself and also that the proper relationship to the natural world is evidence of a positive moral value. Hunting and fishing, then, are not simply ways of testing an isolated man's courage nor his way of keeping sane (as they sometimes appear to be in Hemingway); they are acts meaningful in themselves, like the rising or the setting of the sun. In Miss Gordon's fiction, as in Faulkner's, a man's closeness to nature and his moral sense are closely related. And, conversely, a man's attachment to mere money-making is an index of his depravity. Devotion to an ideal, to a code of honor, is something both writers admire.

So far, I have dealt with Caroline Gordon and the important male writers of this period—for the good reason that these are the writers with whom Miss Gordon appears to have most in common. Since it is customary, when dealing with a woman novelist, to see how she relates to other women writers, it may be of interest to compare her with Katherine Anne Porter, Eudora Welty, and Flannery O'Connor, who are among the best writers of the time. All of them also happen to be Southerners.

In her themes and basic attitudes Miss Gordon has something in common with Eudora Welty, whose career began ten years after Miss Gordon's. In her fiction, Miss Welty is also deeply concerned with what might be called the traditional relationship between the sexes, and she makes the matter of female dominance a crucial issue, particularly in works such as "Petrified Man," *Delta Wedding,* and *The Golden Apples.* Both writers take the traditional view that the man and masculine principles should be dominant and that disorder results when women take control in a society. An important difference is that Miss Welty seems to speak more definitely about her times than Miss Gordon, who is inclined to see the problem as an eternal one. For Miss Welty, it appears (particularly in *The Golden Apples*) that ours is a morganatic society. For Miss Gordon, there have always been women like Cynthia Vail and Vera Claiborne (in *The Malefactors*): those who who want to lead and those who want to be led.

Katherine Anne Porter has an interest in the Southern past, as has Miss Gordon; but ultimately her concern is with the impact of history on the sensibility of her characters, with the personal experience of time. Miss Gordon's interest is very different. Whereas Miss Gordon sees in the Southern past timeless patterns of human experience, Miss Porter (in the novella "Old Morality" and in the short story "The Grave") regards that kind of history as "romantic myth." Eudora Welty, like Caroline Gordon, also sees in present experience repetitions of ancient myth; but, unlike Miss Gordon, she deals in ironic contrast between the heroic qualities of the past and present-day vulgarizations.

With Flannery O'Connor, the youngest of these writers, Miss Gordon shares, in her later fiction, a common religious bond. Both writers are Catholics who deliberately deal with religious themes and subjects. A significant difference between them, however, is that Miss Gordon is somewhat more conscious and more orthodox in her handling of religion. Miss O'Connor often arrives at a traditional religious view by taking a bizzare or violently negative approach; thus, whether intended or not, her fictions can be appreciated by those who do not share her religious convictions and who might even oppose them if her views were overtly presented. On the other hand, Miss Gordon's novel *The Malefactors* and even her story "The Presence" require at least imaginative acceptance of Catholic doctrine for the reader to respond sympathetically. The failure of readers to see or to believe in Thomas Claiborne's religious conversion is a case in point.

Katherine Anne Porter, of course, is also a Catholic; however, her stories that deal with religious themes ("The Jilting of Granny Weatherall" or "Flowering Judas") are much more concerned with the failures experienced by individuals brought up in the Church. The point is not that Miss Porter is rejecting religious faith but that she seems to be exploiting it in order to tell stories with a secular theme.

There are more obvious ways in which Caroline Gordon's work can be related to the fiction of these other women writers. We might point to a common talent for minute observation, which seems a characteristic of the female literary sensibility. We might also mention a concern for family connections, which all of these writers (except Flannery O'Connor) have, though the similarity may be a regional influence; for William Faulkner, a Southerner, is also preoccupied with such relationships, whereas Fitzgerald and Hemingway are not.

What is chiefly noticed, however, when we compare Caroline Gordon's work to that of these other writers are significant differences. Katherine Anne Porter, Eudora Welty, and Flannery O'Connor are openly sensitive, poetic, even occasionally sentimental. Caroline Gordon never is. Indeed, her fiction is sometimes said to lack "warmth" or sentiment. Critics have complained that they have difficulty becoming "involved" with her characters, and the same complaint was made about Henry James and James

Joyce for essentially the same reasons. Caroline Gordon never "lets herself go." She neither brings her emotions directly into a story nor does she openly sympathize with her protagonists. Emotion is what the reader is expected to bring to his reading. The point here, of course, is not that Miss Gordon should have included more sentiment but that it is part of her artistic credo to exclude it; and she has managed to do this so effectively that, as reviewers have noted, it is impossible to tell without looking at the author's name whether her books are written by a man or a woman.

II *Against the Grain*

Caroline Gordon's emotional detachment is but the sign of a deeper detachment which separates her not only from the other important women writers of this period but also from the male writers—even from those with whom she has much in common. For though there are ways in which she can be related to these other novelists, there are significant, perhaps even profound, differences between her and the major writers of this period. Fitzgerald, Faulkner, and Hemingway have their obvious differences; but all three have in common something that Caroline Gordon lacks, moral ambiguity. In the works of these writers the line between good and evil, love and hate, greatness and baseness is usually obscure. Indeed, moral ambiguity is one of the characteristics of our best fiction. Thus, Nick Carraway can say of the hero of *The Great Gatsby*, "I disapproved of him from beginning to end"; but he could also assert "He was a son of God."[2] The impotent protagonist of *The Sun Also Rises*, the moral center of the novel, procures lovers for his sweetheart; and that he does so is presented as a mark of his generosity. The protagonist of *Light in August*, to select one of Faulkner's best novels, is a murderer whose ambiguous color, harsh upbringing, and brutal death transform him into a kind of hero. Miss Gordon's heroes, on the contrary, are traditional both in behavior and in background. This difference may well explain why her fiction has never been very popular either with book buyers or with critics, for popularity feeds on notoriety and perversion as well as on innovation and ambiguity. Modern audiences are willing to applaud goodness if it can be found in a gangster or murderer but not in an obviously good man. For such readers, it seems, such obvious goodness smacks of a conventional morality which is no longer felt to be valid. To make this point in a more elevated way, it might be said that modern audiences can respond to "antiheroes" more readily than to protagonists who act heroically.

Caroline Gordon is perhaps our most unambiguous novelist. She knows what she thinks and how she feels, but she is careful not to let her moral sense distort her representation of reality. Indeed, it seems possible that her techniques for achieving the illusion of objectivity were developed, in part, as a way of keeping her strong moral sense out of sight. Moreover, that popular fictional type, the hero paralyzed by the moral confusion of his world, is not often encountered in her fiction; and, when he does appear, he is not an unwilling victim of external forces but the agent of his own paralysis. Only in *Aleck Maury, Sportsman* and in "Old Red" does she seem morally ambiguous; and, interestingly enough, these works have been her most popular ones.[3] Miss Gordon would probably deny that there are ambiguities in the fictions about Maury; but there is in each a pattern that modern readers have come to expect—the clash of conventional and unconventional behavior and the moral triumph of the latter.

It is curious that Caroline Gordon has not been denounced for creating unambiguous heroes, but has been attacked for not having liberal political and social attitudes.[4] Whether we wish to discuss fiction in these terms or not, it is true that her attitudes and interests, her conception of characters, and her views of social and human relationships are at variance with those held by many readers today. Miss Gordon is well aware of this difference, but that awareness has not kept her from opposing, in her fiction and out, a number of "heresies." Among these might be mentioned the attempt to make women equal with men; the surrender on the part of men of their inherited duty as leaders, their paralysis of the will, and their exalting of the intellect over virtues such as pride, courage, and loyalty; the substitution of self-expression for the mastery of traditional knowledge; and an acquiescence to the more sinister aspects of narcissism.

III *Conclusion*

To say that Caroline Gordon's fiction in its fundamental attitudes runs counter to the drift of our most widely acclaimed writers is not to declare that her work is without its own appeal. On the contrary, her eight novels and two collections of short stories constitute a body of modern American fiction that must be seriously considered. If her beliefs are unusually firm and her emotions unambiguous, she is nevertheless an artist—not a moralist or a propagandist. She exploits her beliefs to make fiction, fiction with subtleties of its own. Instead of ambiguity, she offers what might be called "enigmatic drama." In her narratives, characters move and speak, details about their dress and person are given, and landscapes are conjured up along with farms and houses, horses and automobiles; but we are almost never given an overt clue to what it all means or even what we are to think about any one character. It is as though the author has brought these characters and actions before the reader and then has stood to one side silently looking on.

What we receive from Caroline Gordon's fiction are not large ideas about social, political, or philosophical matters, but a sense of solidly created worlds in which men and women struggle to uphold something that is highly prized. The heroes may be black or white, pioneers or Indians, farmers or soldiers, fishermen or hunters, in times and places that seem rather different from our own; but what counts in her fiction are not differences of color or of time or place but the struggle itself—the ancient, timeless struggle to preserve something of value. Another pleasure derived from Caroline Gordon's novels and stories, one which perhaps only other writers can fully appreciate, is the kind to be had from contemplating what appears, on first glance, to be the most ordinary of subjects and then the discovery, little by little, of the artistic value of every movement, gesture, word. To use an analogy, the kind of pleasure we find is that which a painter might get from studying the canvases of Vermeer or Chardin while the crowds hurry on to view those of El Greco and Picasso.

In present critical esteem, Caroline Gordon may not be regarded as a great writer; but she has created a substantial body of fiction that will continue to give pleasure to those who have the ability to see with their own eyes rather than through the spectacles of currently fashionable dogma. Her fictions have been made to last.

Notes and References

Chapter One

1. My principal source of biographical information is *Twentieth Century Authors*, edited by Stanley J. Kunitz and Howard Haycraft (New York, 1942), and *First Supplement* (New York, 1955). I have also depended to some extent on conversations and written correspondance with Miss Gordon.

2. Louise Cowan, *The Fugitive Group: A Literary History* (Baton Rouge, La., 1954), p. 98.

3. John C. Ransom, *et al.*, *I'll Take My Stand; the South and the Agrarian Tradition* (New York and London, 1930).

4. Miss Gordon has said that she learned a great deal about writing fiction from Mr. Tate.

5. These comments were made by Miss Gordon in a letter to me, May 12, 1965.

6. *Ibid.*

7. This information was supplied by Miss Gordon in a letter to me, May 5, 1968.

8. *Ibid.*

9. "Summer Dust," *Gyroscope*, No. 1 (November, 1929).

10. Sections of this novel have appeared in the *Southern Review*, I New Series (Summer, 1965), 554-69, under the title "Cock Crow," and in the *Transatlantic Review*, XXXI (Winter, 1968-69), 96-113, under the title "A Walk with the Accuser (Who is the God of this World)," and in the *Sewanee Review*, LXVII (Oct.-Dec., 1969), 591-629 under the title "Cloud Nine."

11. For a discussion of Caroline Gordon as a conservative writer, see Chester E. Eisinger, *Fiction of the Forties* (Chicago and London, 1963), pp. 186-93.

12. For a more detailed discussion of Caroline Gordon's relationship with Hemingway and Faulkner see Ch. 12, I.

Chapter Two

1. See John M. Bradbury, *Renaissance in the South: A Critical History of the Literature, 1920-1960* (Chapel Hill, N.C., 1963), pp. 7-21.

2. A statement made by Miss Gordon to me when she was writer-in-residence at Purdue University in 1964.

3. *How to Read a Novel* (New York, 1957), p. 27.
4. *Ibid.*, pp. 24, 227-28.
5. *Ibid.*
6. *Ibid.*
7. *The House of Fiction*, 2nd ed. (New York, 1960), p. 450.
8. *How to Read a Novel*, p. 32.
9. *Ibid.*, pp. 223, 215.
10. *The House of Fiction*, 2nd ed., p. 455.
11. Points Miss Gordon has made in conversation, but see also *The House of Fiction*, p. 190.
12. This is an idea Miss Gordon has taken over from Jacques Maritain. See *How to Read a Novel*, p. 17.
13. *Ibid.*, pp. 208-10 and *The House of Fiction*, pp. 114-15.
14. *How to Read a Novel*, p. 81.
15. *Ibid.*, p. 105.
16. *Ibid.*, p. 107.
17. For Allen Tate's discussion of *Madame Bovary* see "Techniques of Fiction," in *On the Limits of Poetry: Selected Essays, 1928-1948* (New York, 1948), pp. 129-45.
18. *How to Read a Novel*, p. 109.
19. *Ibid.*, p. 110.
20. *Ibid.*, p. 120.
21. *Ibid.*, p. 124.
22. *Ibid.*, p. 125.
23. *Ibid.*, p. 189.
24. *Ibid.*, p. 178.
25. *Ibid.*, p. 223.
26. *Ibid.*, p. 205.
27. *Ibid.*, p. 210.

Chapter Three

1. *Penhally* (New York, 1931), p. 1.
2. For a discussion of the popular family-chronicle novel see W. J. Stuckey, *The Pulitzer Prize Novels* (Norman, Okla., 1966), pp. 33-34, 71-74, 86-89.
3. Frederick P. W. McDowell, *Caroline Gordon* (Minneapolis, Minn., 1966), p. 15.
4. *Penhally*, p. 94.
5. *Ibid.*
6. *Ibid.*, p. 196.
7. *Ibid.*, p. 242.
8. *Ibid.*
9. Ford Madox Ford, "A Stage in American Literature," *Bookman*, LXXIV (December, 1931), 373: "*Penhally* is the best American novel that I know."

Chapter Four

1. *The House of Fiction,* 2nd ed., pp. 439-40. Miss Gordon is here drawing on Henry James's discussion of authority in fiction.
2. For a discussion of this story see Ch. 9.
3. *Aleck Maury, Sportsman* (New York, 1934), p. 84.
4. *Ibid.,* pp. 182-83.
5. *Ibid.,* p. 224.
6. *Ibid.,* pp. 245-53.
7. *Ibid.,* p. 245.
8. *Ibid.,* p. 267.
9. *Ibid.,* p. 278.
10. *Ibid.,* p. 280.
11. *Ibid.*
12. *Ibid.,* p. 281.
13. *Ibid.,* p. 285.
14. Andrew Lytle, "The Forest of the South," *Critique,* I (Winter, 1956), 7.

Chapter Five

1. Certainly the public's preference has been for "costume history" of the kind exemplified by Margaret Mitchell's *Gone With the Wind* and more recently MacKinlay Kantor's *Andersonville,* but in the 1930's T. S. Stribling's anti-romantic views of the Civil War (*The Forge, The Store*) were popular. For a discussion of Civil War fiction, see Robert A. Lively, *Fiction Fights the Civil War.* (Chapel Hill, 1957).
2. Walter Allen, *The Modern Novel in Britain and the United States* (New York, 1964), p. 114.
3. *None Shall Look Back* (New York, 1937), p. 22.
4. The term "code hero" is borrowed from Philip Young's valuable study *Ernest Hemingway* (New York, 1952), p. 36.
5. *None Shall Look Back,* p. 25.
6. *Ibid.,* p. 268.
7. *Ibid.,* p. 347.
8. Allen, *The Modern Novel in Britain and the United States,* p. 114.
9. *None Shall Look Back,* p. 46.
10. *Ibid.*
11. *Ibid.,* p. 42.
12. *Ibid.,* p. 128.
13. *Ibid.,* p. 165.
14. *Ibid.,* p. 66.
15. *Ibid.,* p. 152.
16. *Ibid.,* p. 166.

17. *Ibid.*, p. 171.
18. *Ibid.*, p. 178.
19. *Ibid.*, p. 212.
20. *Ibid.*, p. 217.
21. *Ibid.*, p. 220.
22. *Ibid.*, p. 298.
23. *Ibid.*, p. 285.
24. *Ibid.*, p. 340.
25. *Ibid.*, p. 378.
26. The title of this novel is taken from Nahum: 2.8.

Chapter Six

1. *None Shall Look Back* appeared in February; *The Garden of Adonis*, in October.
2. The epigraph is quoted from the shorter edition of *The Golden Bough* (New York, 1922), p. 341.
3. *Ibid.*, p. 339.
4. *The Garden of Adonis* (New York, 1937), p. 28.
5. *Ibid.*, p. 159.
6. *Ibid.*, p. 271.
7. *Ibid.*
8. See in particular *The Good Earth* (1931) by Pearl Buck and *The Store* (1932) by T. S. Stribling.

Chapter Seven

1. This is a phrase that James uses in a number of places, but see especially his preface to *The Portrait of A Lady* in *The Art of the Novel*, edited by Richard P. Blackmur (New York and London,1948), p. 45.
2. *Green Centuries* (New York, 1941), p. 22.
3. *Ibid.*, pp. 468-69.
4. *Ibid.*, p. 246.
5. *Ibid.*, p. 423. Miss Gordon's quotation is in French: "Je porte en moi la mélancholie des races barbares, avec ses instincts de migrations et ses dégoûts innés de la vie qui leur faisaient quitter leur pays comme pour se quitter eux-mêmes."

Chapter Eight

1. *How to Read a Novel* (New York, 1957), p. 171.
2. *Ibid.*, p. 189.
3. Miss Gordon also diagnoses Gide's difficulties as an advanced stage of narcissism. *Ibid.*, pp. 180-91, 201.

4. *The Women on the Porch* (New York, 1944), p. 316.

5. *Ibid.,* p. 2.

6. *Ibid.,* p. 11.

7. *Ibid.,* p. 260.

8. *Ibid.,* p. 251.

9. *Ibid.*

10. One cause of the failure of the Claibornes' marriage in *The Malefactors* in that Tom Claiborne has failed to rule his wife. See Ch. 10. The moral conflict between the Reardons in *The Strange Children* is dramatized in a physical struggle in which the husband properly restrains his unruly wife. See Ch. 9.

11. *The Women on the Porch,* p. 76.

12. *Ibid.,* p. 220.

13. *Ibid.,* pp. 220-21.

14. *Ibid.,* p. 109.

15. *Ibid.,* pp. 109-10.

16. *Ibid.,* p. 281.

17. *Ibid.,* p. 277.

18. *Ibid.,* p. 130.

19. *Ibid.,* pp. 130-31.

20. *Ibid.,* p. 281.

21. *Ibid.,* p. 286.

22. *Ibid.,* pp. 304-6.

23. *Ibid.,* p. 308.

24. *Ibid.,* pp. 308-9.

25. *How to Read a Novel,* p. 210.

26. *Women on the Porch,* p. 283.

Chapter Nine

1. The abyss or pit is a key image in Miss Gordon's later fiction and criticism, and it generally signifies an undisciplined, disorderly life. Examples, along with related images (such as caves, underground caverns, hollow trees, etc.), are too numerous to catalogue. But see the opening page of *How to Real a Novel* (New York, 1957), in which "decorum" is called the "thin ice on which we must all skate if we are not to fall into the abyss that yawns for each of us."

2. See Ch. 11, X.

3. *The Women on the Porch* (New York, 1941), p. 316.

4. *The Strange Children* (New York, 1951), p. 17.

5. In some ways Lucy also resembles Undine. Her mother refers to her as a "sort of changeling" (*ibid.,* p. 54), and she is attracted to Uncle Tubby, is capricious, "gains a soul" but, unlike Undine, she is saved from the underworld life."

6. *Ibid.,* p. 227.

7. *Ibid.,* p. 156.

8. *Ibid.*, p. 302.

9. *Ibid.*, p. 129.

10. *Ibid.*, p. 131.

11. *Ibid.*, pp. 163-64.

12. *Ibid.*, p. 220.

13. *Ibid.*, p. 258.

14. *Ibid.*, p. 127.

15. *Ibid.*

16. *Ibid.*, p. 129.

17. *Ibid.*, p. 303.

18. *Ibid.*

Chapter Ten

1. At the time of this writing, Miss Gordon is at work on her ninth novel which is to be entitled *A Narrow Heart: The Portrait of A Woman*. Three sections of this have been published in periodicals. See Note 10, Ch. 1, for details of publication.

2. *The Malefactors* (New York, 1956), p. 76.

3. *Ibid.*, p. 268.

4. *Ibid.*, p. 312.

5. *Ibid.*, p. 172.

6. *Ibid.*, p. 173.

7. *Ibid.*, p. 168.

8. This point is made later when George Crenfew tells Tom that he, George, "would never have amounted to a damn if it hadn't been for" Claiborne's father who taught him "about the heroes." *Ibid.*, p. 276.

9. *Ibid.*, p. 78.

10. *Ibid.* See also pp. 245-48.

11. *Ibid.*, p. 163.

12. *Ibid.*, p. 232.

13. *Ibid.*, pp. 232-40.

14. John B. Bradbury, *Renaissance in the South: A Critical History of the Literature, 1920-1960* (Chapel Hill, N.C., 1963), p. 62.

15. This identification was made by Miss Gordon in conversation, 1964.

16. Bradbury, p. 62.

17. *The Malefactors*, p. 76.

18. *Ibid.*, p. 74.

19. *Ibid.*, p. 236.

20. Miss Gordon made this comment in a seminar at Purdue University in 1965.

21. *The Malefactors*, p. 42.

22. See especially her comments on André Gide, *How to Read a Novel*, pp. 208-10, and her story based on Gide's life, "Emmanuele!

Emmanuele!" in *Old Red and Other Stories,* pp. 26-68. See also Ch. 11, VII.

23. *The Malefactors,* p. 66.

24. *Ibid.,* p. 41.

25. *Ibid.,* p. 42.

26. *Ibid.*

27. *Ibid.,* p. 185.

28. *Ibid.,* p. 184.

29. *Ibid.,* p. 126.

30. *Ibid.,* p. 298.

31. *Ibid.,* p. 100.

32. These writers are more direct in some works than in others, but the religious implications are often missed, ignored, or inverted by critics.

Chapter Eleven

1. A statement made by Miss Gordon in conversation with me in 1964.

2. There are many passing references to Miss Gordon's talent for short fiction, but see especially Ray B. West, Jr., *The Short Story in America: 1900-1950* (Chicago, 1952), p. 76; John M. Bradbury, *Renaissance in the South: A Critical History of the Literature, 1920-1960* (Chapel Hill, N.C., 1963), p. 63; Frederick P. W. McDowell, *Caroline Gordon* (Minneapolis, Minn., 1966); p. 11.

3. *The Forest of the South* (New York, 1945), p. 147.

4. In a letter to Robert and Constance Hunting, June 20, 1966, Miss Gordon wrote: "I have always felt that one of the reasons 'The Captive' is such a good story is that so much of the work had already been done for me. I had only to build on Connelley's foundation." See William Elsey Connelley, *Eastern Kentucky Papers: The Founding of Harman's Station with an account of the Indian captivity of Mrs. Jennie Wiley. . . .* (New York, 1910).

5. A comment made by Miss Gordon in conversation with me in 1964.

6. *The Forest of the South,* p. 105.

7. *Ibid.,* p. 119.

8. *Ibid.,* p. 122.

9. *Ibid.,* p. 123.

10. *Ibid.,* p. 124.

11. *Ibid.,* p. 128.

12. *Ibid.,* p. 114.

13. *Ibid.,* p. 115.

14. *Ibid.,* p. 118.

15. *Ibid.,* p. 110.

16. It is ironic that "Old Red'" should have taken the second O. Henry prize, but not, therefore, surprising that the character of Aleck Maury should have been completely misunderstood by the judges. See Introduction, *O. Henry Memorial Award Prize Stories of 1934*, ed., Harry Hansen, (Garden City, N.Y., 1934), p. xi.

17. *The Forest of the South*, p. 158.

18. *Ibid.*, p. 205.

19. McDowell, *Caroline Gordon*, pp. 11-12, fails to see that the narrator is to be viewed ironically and therefore misses the point of the story which is about Tom Doty's heroism.

20. *The Forest of the South*, p. 240.

21. *Ibid.*, p. 85.

22. *Ibid.*

23. Jonathan Daniels, *Saturday Review of Literature*, XXVIII (October 27, 1945), 40.

24. Andrew Nelson Lytle, "The Forest of the South," *Critique*, I (Winter, 1956), 7.

25. *The Forest of the South*, p .77.

26. *Ibid.*

27. *Ibid.*, p. 78.

28. *Ibid.*

29. *Ibid.*

30. *Lytle*, p. 7.

31. *The Forest of the South*, p. 82.

32. *Ibid.*

33. *Ibid.*

34. *Ibid.*, p. 224.

35. *Ibid.*, p. 229.

36. *Ibid.*

37. *Ibid.*, p. 239.

38. "Caroline Gordon and the Historic Image," *Sewanee Review*, LVII (Autumn, 1949), pp. 562-67.

39. *The Forest of the South*, p. 183.

40. *Ibid.*, p. 182.

41. *Ibid.*, p. 188.

42. *Ibid.*

43. *Ibid.*, p. 189.

44. *Ibid.*, p. 190.

45. *Ibid.*, p. 194.

46. See Section X, this chapter.

47. The portrait of Gide in Fäy will be clear to anyone familiar with the facts of Gide's life. Miss Gordon said that this story was suggested to her by an account of Gide's behavior in North Africa told her by a young American professor.

48. *Old Red and Other Stories* (New York, 1963), p. 68.

49. R. V. Cassill, "New Fiction," N.Y. *Herald Tribune Book Week,* Oct. 20, 1963, p. 22.

50. *Old Red and Other Stories,* p. 170.

51. *Ibid.,* p. 174.

52. *Ibid.,* p. 186.

53. *Ibid.*

54. *Ibid.,* p. 185.

55. *Ibid.,* p. 183.

56. *Ibid.,* p. 123.

57. *Ibid.,* p. 23.

Chapter Twelve

1. A remark made about the neglect in their day of Hawthorne, Flaubert, and Henry James. *How to Read a Novel* (New York, 1953), p. 228.

2. F. Scott Fitzgerald, *The Great Gatsby* (Scribner's Students' Edition) (New York, 1953), p. 99.

3. Whenever one of Caroline Gordon's novels is singled out for praise, it is usually *Aleck Maury, Sportsman.* See Ray B. West, Jr., *The Short Story in America, 1900-1950* (Chicago, 1952), p. 76; Frederick J. Hoffman, "Caroline Gordon: The Special Yield," *Critique,* I (Winter, 1956), p. 34; Howard Baker, "The Contemporary Short Story," III, *Southern Review* (Winter, 1938), p. 595; William Van O'Connor, "Art and Miss Gordon's Style," in *The Grotesque: An American Genre and Other Essays* (Carbondale, Ill., 1962), p. 171.

4. See Chester E. Eisinger, *Fiction of the Forties* (Chicago and London, 1963), pp. 186-93, and Walter Allen, *The Modern Novel in Britain and the United States* (New York, 1964), p. 114.

Selected Bibliography

PRIMARY SOURCES

1. Novels
Penhally. New York: Charles Scribner's Sons, 1931.
Aleck Maury, Sportsman. New York: Charles Scribner's Sons, 1934.
None Shall Look Back. New York: Charles Scribner's Sons, 1937.
The Garden of Adonis. New York: Charles Scribner's Sons, 1937.
Green Centuries. New York: Charles Scribner's Sons, 1941.
The Women on the Porch. New York: Charles Scribner's Sons, 1944.
The Strange Children. New York: Charles Scribner's Sons, 1951.
The Malefactors. New York, Harcourt, Brace and Company, 1956.
2. Short Story Collections
The Forest of the South. New York: Charles Scribner's Sons, 1945.
Old Red and Other Stories. New York: Charles Scribner's Sons, 1963.
3. Other Volumes
The House of Fiction: An Anthology of the Short Story, with commentary by Caroline Gordon and Allen Tate. New York: Charles Scribner's Sons, 1950; second edition, 1960.
How to Read a Novel. New York: Viking Press, Inc., 1957.
A Good Soldier: A Key to the Novels of Ford Madox Ford. Davis: University of California Library, 1963.
4. Other Writings
Contribution to "Homage to Ford Madox Ford—A Symposium," *New Directions* 7, New York, 1942.
"Mr. Faulkner's Southern Saga," *New York Times Book Review* (April 5, 1956), p. 45.
"Notes on Faulkner and Flaubert," *Hudson Review*, I (Summer, 1948), 22-31.
"Stephen Crane," *Accent*, IX (Spring, 1949), 153-57.
"Notes on Hemingway and Kafka," *Sewanee Review*, LVII (Spring, 1949), 215-26.
"Notes on Chekhov and Maugham," *Sewanee Review*, LVII (Summer, 1949), 401-10.
"The Art and Mystery of Faith," *Newman Annual* (Minneapolis), 1953, pp. 55-62.
"A Virginian in Prairie Country," *New York Times Book Review* (March 8, 1953), pp. 1, 31.
"Some Readings and Misreadings," *Sewanee Review*, LXI (1953), 384-407.

"The Story of Ford Madox Ford," *Highlights of Modern Literature: A Permanent Collection of Memorable Essays from the New York Times Book Review,* edited by Francis Brown. A Mentor Book. New York: The New American Library, 1954.

"Mr. Verver, Our National Hero," *Sewanee Review,* LXIII (Winter, 1955), 29-47.

"Flannery O'Connor's Wise Blood," *Critique,* II (Fall, 1958), 3-10.

"The Novels of Brainard Cheney," *Sewanee Review,* LXVII (Spring, 1959), 322-30.

SECONDARY SOURCES

ALLEN, WALTER. *The Modern Novel in Britain and the United States.* New York: E. P. Dutton & Co., Inc., 1964, pp. 113-14. Discusses *None Shall Look Back.*

BLUM, MORGAN. "The Shifting Point of View: Joyce's 'The Dead' and Gordon's 'Old Red,' " *Critique,* I (Winter, 1956), 45-66. Discusses reasons for the principle techniques of "Old Red."

BRADBURY, JOHN M. *Renaissance in the South: A Critical History of the Literature, 1920-1960.* Chapel Hill: University of North Carolina Press, 1964. Brief summaries of the novels with an estimate of successes and failures that are sometimes perceptive.

BROWN, ASHLEY. "The Novel as Christian Comedy." *Reality and Myth: Essays in American Literature in Honor of Richard Croom Beatty.* Edited by William E. Walker and Robert L. Walker. Nashville, Tenn.: Vanderbilt University Press, 1964. Draws a number of significant parallels between Dante's *Divine Comedy* and *The Malefactors.*

————. "The Achievement of Caroline Gordon." *Southern Humanities Review,* II (1968), 279-90. An over-view of Caroline Gordon's career as a literary figure.

CHENEY, BRAINARD. "Caroline Gordon's Ontological Quest," *Renascence,* XVI (Fall, 1963), 3-12. Regards *The Malefactors* as the end toward which all of Caroline Gordon's fiction was moving. Makes a persuasive defense of the convincing quality of Claiborne's religious conversion.

COWAN, LOUISE. "Nature and Grace in Caroline Gordon." *Critique,* I (Winter, 1956), 11-27. A perceptive discussion of Miss Gordon's handling of man's relation to nature and the relationship of men and women.

EISINGER, CHESTER E. *Fiction of the Forties.* Chicago: University of Chicago Press, 1964. Discusses Miss Gordon's fiction as the product of a conservative imagination.

FLETCHER, MARIE. "The Fate of Women in a Changing South: A Persistent Theme in the Fiction of Caroline Gordon," *Mississippi Quarterly*, XXI (1968), 17-28. Focuses on the problem of being a woman in the South.

FORD, FORD MADOX. "A Stage in American Literature," *Bookman*, LXXIV (December, 1931), 371-76. Ford uses *Penhally* as an example of the high quality of the new American fiction.

GRISCOM, JOAN. "Bibliography of Caroline Gordon," *Critique*, I (Winter, 1956), 74-78. Incomplete, but useful.

HEILMAN, ROBERT B. "School for Girls," *Sewanee Review*, LX (Spring, 1952), 299-309. A perceptive review of *The Strange Children*.

HOFFMAN, FREDERICK J. "Caroline Gordon: The Special Yield," *Critique*, I (Winter, 1956), 29-35. Argues that the novel and the stories about Aleck Maury are the best and "most illuminating" of Miss Gordon's thematic concerns. Briefly mentions successes and failures in her fiction.

KING, LAWRENCE T. "The Novels of Caroline Gordon," *Catholic World*, CLXXXI (July, 1955), 274-79. Résumés of several novels.

KOCH, VIVIENNE. The "Forest of the South," *Sewanee Review*, LIV (July-September, 1946), 543-47. A perceptive review of *The Forest of the South*.

————. "The Conservatism of Caroline Gordon." *The Southern Renascence*, edited by Louis D. Rubin and Robert D. Jacobs. Baltimore: Johns Hopkins University Press, 1953. Deals with the fiction through *Strange Children*, emphasizing the Southern qualities and the "naturalism." Perceptive.

LYTLE, ANDREW N. "Caroline Gordon and the Historic Image," *Sewanee Review*, LVII (Autumn, 1949), 560-86. Longest and most useful article on Miss Gordon's fiction, but it suffers somewhat from an attempt to make everything fit a too simple thesis.

————. "The Forest of the South," *Critique*, I (Winter, 1956), 3-9. Sees "the stress between the sexes" as the main subject of Miss Gordon's fiction, a thesis that obliges him to ignore the themes of individual stories and novels.

McDOWELL, FREDERICK P. W. *Caroline Gordon*. Minneapolis, Minn.: University of Minnesota Press, 1966. Pamphlet No. 59 in the University of Minnesota Pamphlets on American Writers. Summaries of the novels with occasional critical comments and brief mention of some of the short stories.

O'CONNOR, WILLIAM VAN. "Art and Miss Gordon." *The Grotesque: An American Genre and Other Essays*. Carbondale: Southern Illinois University Press, 1962. A useful discussion of Caroline Gordon's art.

ROCK, JAMES E. "The Christian Myth as Salvation: Caroline Gordon's *The Strange Children*, *Tulane Studies in English*, XVI (1968), 149-60. An extended discussion of *Strange Children* along with a brief look at earlier fiction.

————. "The Mind and Art of Caroline Gordon," *Mississippi Quar-*

terly, XXI (1968), 1-16. An interesting interpretation of Caroline Gordon's fiction.

Ross, DANFORTH. "Caroline Gordon's Golden Ball," *Critique*, I (Winter, 1956), 67-73. Former student of Miss Gordon describes her classroom manner and a number of her fictional principles.

RUBIN, LARRY. "Christian Allegory in Caroline Gordon's 'The Captive,'" *Studies in Short Fiction*, V (Spring, 1968), 283-89. Argues that the story reflects a Christian vision of damnation and salvation.

SULLIVAN, WALTER. "Southern Novelists and the Civil War." *The Southern Renascence*. Edited by Louis D. Rubin and Robert D. Jacobs. Baltimore: Johns Hopkins University Press, 1953. Brief but perceptive comment on *None Shall Look Back*.

THORP, WILLARD. "The Way Back and the Way Up: The Novels of Caroline Gordon," *Bucknell Review*, VI (December, 1956), 1-15. Informed, sympathetic discussion of her novels.

Index

DATE DUE
REMINDER

APR 10 '97

Please do not remove
this date due slip.